SECRETS
OF THE
PARADOX

SOLVING THE LIAR
OTHER LOGICAL PROBLEMS

SECRETS

OF THE

PARADOX

SOLVING THE LIAR
AND OTHER LOGICAL PROBLEMS

MICHEAL D. WINTERBURN

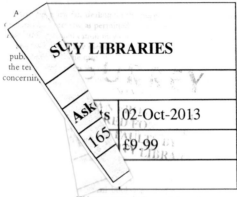

Web: www.troubador.co.uk/matador

ISBN 978 1783060 269

British Library Cataloguing in Publication Data.
A catalogue record for this book is available from the British Library.

Typeset in Aldine401 BT Roman by Troubador Publishing Ltd
Printed and bound in the UK by TJ International, Padstow, Cornwall

Matador is an imprint of Troubador Publishing Ltd

To the memory of Raymund Andrea
1882 – 1975

CONTENTS

FIGURES AND TABLES

PREFACE

My formal introduction to paradox occurred a little over thirty years ago when I purchased the very slim anthology, *Vicious Circles and Infinity*. It was packed with all manner of fascinating problems which I quickly discovered had the power to inflict severe mental torment. My first attempt to crack one of these mind-manglers took place shortly afterwards, when I made a few notes on the paradox of Achilles and the Tortoise. I can't recall exactly when it was I decided that, one day, I should like to write a book that aimed to solve various paradoxes, but it must have been round about that time. What I do remember is that, in my youthful enthusiasm, I had decided to call it *Death of the Paradox*. I firmly believed then, as indeed I do now, that a paradox exists only because we are ignorant of all the faulty elements that contribute to it, and that once these defects have been fully identified the paradox will simply evaporate and exist no more. We will have explained it away.

What I also remember is that in those days I never really attempted to solve any of the major paradoxes with any seriousness. For some reason I confidently believed that I would be able to find solutions, but I also believed it was pointless going ahead if I was unable to solve the most difficult of them all, the Liar ('This statement is false.' If the statement is true, it is false; if it is false, it is true). The way I looked at it, a book which claimed to solve several of the major paradoxes, but which did not include the Liar, would be only second best. However useful such a book might prove to be, it would contain an implicit admission of defeat: that the Liar was just too difficult for the writer to solve.

I wanted to solve the Liar, but I couldn't. I couldn't make any progress with it at all. This perhaps should not have been a source of frustration for me, since no one else had come anywhere near unlocking its secrets in over two and a half thousand years, and yet it was.

Meanwhile, I was getting on with my life in one way and another and thoughts about paradoxes began to occupy me only intermittently. Then I went to university – rather late – and in the library came across *The Paradoxicon*, a splendid anthology for the general reader, which reignited my enthusiasm for all things paradoxical. In a very minor way I also encountered Gödel's work for the first time, and in years to come this was to prove invaluable to me (in order to fully explain the Liar I am compelled to call upon and reinterpret certain aspects of Gödel's achievement). Though my degree studies were taking me in a somewhat different direction, I somehow gained permission to write a dissertation on a particular type of paradox. I reproduce this here in two parts, slightly adapted for the different format, as *The Unexpected Examination* and *The Unexpected Egg*.

Years went by, and though they were never very far from my mind, I rarely sat down and attempted anything else to do with paradoxes. Whenever I did, it was solely to the Liar that I turned. I still had the desire to write a book, yet still was determined not to attempt one that did not include this king of the paradoxes. Only if I could solve the Liar would I take a look at some of the others.

But I could never get anywhere. The Liar seemed impenetrable, impregnable. It was like a city with a very high, very thick, very smooth perimeter wall that could not be scaled and could not be breached. Applying the closest of scrutiny whilst endlessly walking around it would never reveal even the slightest chink. What was going on inside this city could never be known. Perhaps it was full of life and exuberant activity? Perhaps it was deserted and desolate? Unless I could find a gap in the wall through which some light shone out, or through which I could shine light in, I would never, ever know. The Liar remained defiantly uncommunicative.

Then, in the summer of 2006, I had a breakthrough. I had just begun reading *Wittgenstein's Poker* when I felt the sudden urge to have another go at the Liar. I made some exploratory jottings, fiddled about with a few ideas, and after an hour or two there came the insight that truth and falsity belong in a proposition's *future*, not in its present.

This was all I needed. This was the gap in the wall that I had for so long been searching. For the next two weeks, night and day, I obsessively wrote page after page of notes as I mentally dug my way inside the Liar and several other paradoxes. Some of these notes were of little value, some of my meandering conclusions were wrong, but this exercise in sustained deep thought ultimately proved very productive and eventually grew into the work that is now before you.

So what *is* a paradox? Its most common features are self-reference, contradiction and vicious circularity. R. M Sainsbury believes a paradox is '… an apparently unacceptable conclusion derived by apparently acceptable reasoning from apparently acceptable premises'. Not everyone is totally happy with this definition, and perhaps it doesn't cover every nuance of every paradox, but it's good enough to satisfy most people, including me. For Roy Sorensen, 'Paradoxes mark fault lines in our common-sense world'. I have characterised them as 'logical logjams', a very clumsy expression for a very clumsy state of affairs. Whatever the attempt at a definition, each one goes some way towards suggesting that paradoxes do something that is very wrong and by and large have us all stumped.

In this book I have been little concerned about any wider philosophical or logical implications that solutions to the Liar or any of the other paradoxes may entail. That many paradoxes have stalled the onward progress of thought and called into question some long-cherished laws of logic has been challenge enough for me.

I examine nine paradoxes and suggest new ways of approaching them. For paradoxes 1 to 7, I believe I have achieved solutions (or perhaps *resolutions* would be more accurate). For numbers 8 and 9, because they are more the province of scientific rather than logical enquiry, I merely offer a few thoughts that I believe are pertinent to each of the problems.

Occasionally, it has been necessary to coin new words in order to express novel ideas. Here and there I identify a new principle, pattern or formula that I believe is either causing the paradox or will contribute towards its solution. Throughout, my watchwords have been clarity, simplicity and readability. Paradoxes are inherently difficult, so I have striven to add a touch of lightness from time to time and to guide the reader gently over any rough terrain. I have tried my best to explain everything in plain English, and therefore you will not find any troublesome technical terms or specialist logical notation here. Additionally, I have included tables, diagrams and analogies where I thought they might aid or enhance understanding. In truth, I have written the type of philosophy book that, given a choice, I personally would like to read and my hope is that its style will also appeal to you.

Nevertheless, it must be said that *Secrets of the Paradox* will make certain intellectual demands of the reader; but if you are prepared for that and relish that, and if I have done my job well enough, then I am sure everything will be fine. It is anticipated that the book will be fully accessible by those who have a general interest, whilst also being sufficiently rigorous to satisfy the demands of the professional philosopher.

It may be asked why I have placed the Liar paradox first and not left the best to the last, as it were. Well, I reckon that wherever I might place it, it would be the section that most people decide to read first, simply because of its lofty status: if we are at all interested in paradoxes then this is the one we are the most eager to get to the bottom of. Also, my analysis of the Liar gave rise to certain principles which I subsequently discovered in, or applied to, some of the other paradoxes, and so it is fitting that the Liar comes first. Indeed, it is for this very reason that the Liar *should* be read first. Nevertheless, while the Liar may well deserve its star-billing, I am confident you will find many other fine acts in the show, each with their own peculiar talents and attractions.

I do believe that in this book the Liar has been solved. Certainly, it has been solved to my own satisfaction, and I try to set the bar fairly high in regard to my levels of logical contentment. By 'solved', I mean that it has been thoroughly explained away and as a consequence has lost its power of paradox. That is not to say that I think the very last word has been said, that the Liar has been entirely exhausted of its secrets. It has not: the more thought that is given to this or any other paradox, the more discoveries there are to be made in regard to them (indeed, at the end of the book, I present several peripheral questions/problems which have arisen and which some readers may wish to attempt to answer for themselves). But I do believe that nothing more of substance will be found that could materially add to our understanding of the main causes of contradiction within the Liar.

What I am certain of is that the Liar has been inadequately labelled a *semantic* paradox. It is far more than that. Truth and falsity are obviously central to the problem, but it is within the structure and life-cycle of a proposition that we shall find our real answers. Time, sequence, human psychology and other factors will also have prominent parts to play. In addressing the Liar, the boundary between logic and science became blurred and was occasionally crossed.

Russell's paradox is one of the most important paradoxes of modern times and simply *had* to be addressed. Similarly, the Barber of Seville, which is intimately connected to it. Surprisingly, Sainsbury dismisses the Barber as insignificant, awarding it a lowly one mark out of ten on his scale of difficulty. His argument is that such a barber could not possibly exist. However, my own analysis would suggest that he has done this paradox a disservice, because in reality it is rich in illuminating insights. It is not good enough summarily to brush aside a paradox when it is screaming out to be explained. I would place the Barber of Seville far higher up on Sainsbury's scale.

The Crocodile's Dilemma has always struck me as a fun sort of paradox, though it wouldn't be much fun were it to occur for real! I chose to explore it because of this fun aspect, but also because it throws up some difficulties that test us in ways that are different to many other paradoxes.

Achilles and the Tortoise was, as I have mentioned, the first paradox that I ever worked on, and it is partly as a nod to my younger self that I address it again here. I have based much of my analysis on the notes that I made all those years ago and believe there may be one or two things of interest that may contribute towards a better understanding of this problem. The 'unexpected' paradoxes (which, it occurred to me only very recently, contain the seeds of the solution to the Liar) I include for similar reasons. All of these are important paradoxes and there is much we can learn from them.

I suspect that my decision to consider premonitions may cause a few eyebrows to be raised, or eyes to be rolled, amongst the purists. But a paradox is a paradox wherever it is to be found and should always be worthy of our attention. Besides, it takes us into completely different territory to most other paradoxes and sometimes it is good to break free of our usual constraints. Additionally, it allows me to probe into areas that have been a source of interest to me for very many years. I cannot claim to offer a full and tidy solution to this paradox, yet I do feel that I offer some observations that will be of value to those who work in this field

The last paradox in the book is about time travel. Now I really am on shaky ground! I know little advanced physics, but couldn't resist an opportunity to chew over this difficult problem. *Is* time travel possible? I suspect not, but I really couldn't say. Logic and reason alone are underequipped to answer this question, and yet I do think they may be able to offer a few items of note. So I shall be more or less arguing against time travel whilst at the same time keeping a wary eye open for something that kicks my arguments into oblivion. Well, it's okay to speculate, isn't it? After all, even physics does not have all the answers yet and is itself obliged to speculate pending further developments – so it seems I am in good company.

I have tried to eliminate all error from my work, but it may be that I have tripped up here and there without realizing it; I therefore seek your pardon in advance for any imperfections you may discover.

Finally, I hope you will soon join me in the realm of paradox, for many wonderful secrets await you there!

THE LIAR

A SNEAK PREVIEW OF SOME OF THE SECRETS

Some Very Important Characters

You are in conversation with an athlete in the Olympic stadium. She will be running in tomorrow's final of the 100 metres. She asks, 'Will I win the race?' You reply that you don't know, that you both shall just have to wait and see, yet you wish her good luck. This athlete's name is Interrogative Sentence, or Question to her friends.

A short while later and you are speaking with another athlete, who is also a 100 metres finalist. She tells you, 'I'm going to win.' You admire her self-confidence and think that, yes, she may indeed win, though with the result of the race yet to be determined you realize that her confidence may be misplaced. Her name is Declarative Sentence, but most people call her Proposition.

Another athlete approaches you. She, too, will be competing in tomorrow's 100 metres final. She boasts, 'I have won the race,' and asserts that she has already been awarded the gold medal, which is in her tracksuit pocket. When you protest that she has yet to run the race, so she cannot possibly have already won it, she insists that she is definitely the 100 metres Olympic champion. You are somewhat puzzled and confused, yet reluctant to get into an argument with this woman, since in every other respect she does seem perfectly sane and normal. So you take her at her word, even though you can't understand how she could possibly be the gold medallist a day in advance of the race. You decide that, if she really does have the gold medal in her pocket, right here and now, and it is inscribed with all the details of the event and also with her name, then she must indeed be the champion, as strange as that may seem. If, on the other hand, there is no medal, then she definitely is not the champion. She doesn't offer to show you it, yet insists that she does have it.

You are desperate to know if there actually is a gold medal in this athlete's pocket, but the only thing she reveals is an enigmatic smile which drives you mad. Is she or isn't she the 100 metres champion? You tell yourself – rather firmly – that this third athlete cannot have already won the race, but the trouble is, you are certain that you have this very second glimpsed the gold medal in her pocket. So she must be the champion. But she can't be. Yet she must be. But she can't be … you are driven to despair!

This athlete's name is Liar Paradox. She is said to suffer from vicious circularity: perhaps this is an awful disease that has unbalanced her mind – and is now beginning to infect yours …

You have heard about the possibility of speaking to a fourth athlete, but she is unavailable today. When you put in an official request to interview her you are given the reply that this can only take place after tomorrow's 100 metres final. When you politely insist on seeing her today, here and now, you are respectfully told that it would be impossible to meet her. You demand to know why and are told that she will not even exist until the race has ended. You are baffled. To help you out a little, the Olympic Games official tells you that, though this woman looks, dresses and acts like an athlete, she is actually only a commentator on the race. That's her proper job, though lots of people mistakenly think she is one of the finalists. Her name is Verification Statement.

You are warned, however, that you need to be on your guard when listening to her, because, though her job is to report on the race, she doesn't always get her facts straight. Sometimes she tells the truth about who the real winner was, but sometimes she tells lies. She's the spitting image of the athlete known as Proposition. They could almost be twins. You are further told that you can never really work out whether Verification Statement is telling the truth or telling a lie, and that the only way you can ever know for certain who won the race is to *watch the race yourself*. 'What good is a commentator if you can't trust what she tells you?' you ask. All you receive from the official is a shrug of the shoulders.

Just as you think you have enough puzzles to cope with, along comes another athlete and says to you, 'I am running in the women's 100 metres final tomorrow, but no matter how hard I try, nor how long I keep on running, I shall never be able to cross the finishing line.' Now you are thoroughly bamboozled. This doesn't make any sense at all! When you ask her to explain *why* she will never be able to finish the race, she says it is because the finishing line will always retreat from her whenever and however she approaches it. You remark that you think this is grossly unfair, bearing in mind that the race is supposed to be run over a fixed distance, and that surely this must be an infringement of the rules. Yet this athlete merely issues a sigh of resignation. Her name is Gödel Sentence and her professional life is one of unresolved and unrelieved frustration.

These five characters embody many of the problems associated with the puzzle known as the Epimenides, or Liar, paradox. Two of them are quite ordinary and familiar, while the other three are, I think you would agree, more than a touch peculiar. In order to arrive at some kind of a solution for this paradox, it is necessary that we become better acquainted with each of them and find out what makes them tick.

But first, another secret …

The True/False Trichotomy

True and false are polar opposites and there are only three possible permutations of statements that can be made in regard to these pairs. I have named this trio the true/false trichotomy.

STATEMENT	TYPE	STATUS
(a) Either true or false	PROPOSITION	CONSISTENT
(b) Neither true nor false	GÖDEL SENTENCE	NEUTRAL
(c) Both true and false	LIAR PARADOX	INCONSISTENT

1. The true/false trichotomy

It can be seen from the above that I believe there are *three* types of statement, and that a proposition is but one of them. A proposition is a statement which must have the capacity to be either true or false. Statement type (a) describes, or is a blueprint for, a proposition.

With statement type (b), I would contend that this is the blueprint for an alternative form of the Gödel sentence, 'This statement cannot be proved or disproved', for reasons that I shall argue in due course. I shall not be classifying the Gödel sentence as true but unprovable, which is the common response to it, but as *neutral*. It cannot be true. It cannot be false. Yet it most assuredly does exist and is valid as a statement, though *not* as a proposition.

In statement type (c) we encounter the Liar paradox, where true and false states apparently co-exist, but in fierce opposition to one another. But they cannot co-exist if the classical laws of logic are to remain intact. So (c) is inadmissible. Or is it? There are some thinkers today who believe that in some circumstances we should begin to challenge the laws of logic and accept contradiction. I am not one of them. It will gradually become clear why I am not. I intend to demonstrate that statement type (c) also is neutral with regard to truth-value – it, too, is neither true nor false and it, too, is *not* a proposition.

Should any of the above assertions seem to run counter to commonly held opinion, I would ask that you bear with me: in working towards a solution for the Liar paradox I shall be arguing *in support* of commonly held opinion, but modifying it somewhat, as I do not believe it to be sufficiently comprehensive. We have not yet been given the full story.

Incidentally, in mathematics there is the proven law of trichotomy which states that every real number must be either positive, negative or zero. It is my contention that the true/false trichotomy mirrors this mathematical law, with its two polar opposites of true and false [positive and negative] and neutral [zero]. Were we to substitute these three number types for the terms in our present trichotomy, we would discover a correspondence:

(a) Either positive or negative	NUMBER	CONSISTENT
(b) Neither positive nor negative	ZERO	NEUTRAL
(c) Both positive and negative	PARADOX	INCONSISTENT

2. Numbers and the true/false trichotomy

It would appear, then, that there is a fundamental parallel between the types of statements and numbers that can exist, and that this must have its basis in natural law. In (c) above, however, perhaps mathematicians would not call this clash of positive and negative 'paradox', but come to a different conclusion: that a positive and negative number of equal value cancel each other out to become neutral, or zero (eg. -1 + 1 = 0). I shall be reaching the same conclusion in regard to paradoxical statements, that they too become neutral (and not nonsensical, as some have argued).

Observe also how positive, negative and neutral particles (the proton, electron and neutron) are fundamental components of the atom. How a bar magnet, with its polar opposites of North and South, has a neutral zone at its centre. Wherever polar opposites are to be found in the natural world, so, too, will a neutral zone be in evidence that separates the two and mediates between them. It is my contention that statements follow this very same pattern.

In attempting to unravel and solve the Liar paradox, which is the toughest paradox of them all, we shall be obliged to look closely at what constitutes a proposition and discuss how Gödel comes to be involved in all of this. We shall reinforce the prevailing view that the Gödel sentence is unique, special, and it will command a very prominent place in our journey of discovery.

Introducing the Liar Paradox

The Liar is of ancient Greek origin and has been called the granddaddy of all paradoxes. Originally devised by the philosopher Eubulides in the 6th century B.C., a famous ancient version runs as follows:

> Epimenides, the Cretan, says, 'All Cretans are liars.' If he is telling the truth he is lying; and if he is lying he is telling the truth.

As it stands, this version of the paradox is inadequate, for the simple reason that it is too easy to wriggle out of, thus eliminating the paradox. An analysis could run something like this:

Epimenides says *all* Cretans are liars. *All* Cretans assumes an intimate knowledge of all other Cretans alive, which it is doubtful he will have, unless he is the *only* Cretan or one of but a few. Yet, let us assume he does have such knowledge.

(1) Cretans may well be liars *some* of the time, yet not *all* of the time, hence they are still liars, so the statement is true, but *without* the paradoxical retort; for he, as a Cretan, may be telling the truth on this occasion, without contradicting his statement.

(2) 'All Cretans are liars *all* of the time.' This tightens up the paradox and makes it very difficult to wriggle out of.

(3) We must reduce again to 'Every statement I make is a lie'. This gets all other Cretans out of the way (apologies!) and allows us to concentrate on Epimenides alone, whilst retaining the paradox. But 'Every statement I make is a lie' assumes that Epimenides knows he will continue to tell *nothing but* lies in the future. Can he be so sure of this?

(4) In essence, the statement is declaring: (a) 'All my past statements were false', (b) 'This statement is false', and (c) 'All my future statements will be false'. Does this Cretan have total self-knowledge? Can he be certain that every statement he made in the past was false? And that every future statement he makes will be false?

(5) Let us take statement (a), 'All my past statements were false'. If Epimenides once upon a time said, 'I am a soldier', when in fact he was a sailor, then he was lying. If he once said, 'I had kippers for breakfast this morning', when in reality he had two poached eggs on toast, he was lying. We can, then, see the possibility (though perhaps not the probability) that he has always in the past lied about everything, and knows this. So we can dismiss statement (a) as conceivably true, but without the paradox, since it is referring to past statements, not the present statement.

(6) Now statement (b), 'This statement is false'. This presents a terrible difficulty. It is a real stinker, and the cause of centuries of brainache and heartache. It can undermine everything we are saying about statements (a) and (c), reducing our analysis to

gobbledegook. We shall be compelled to return to this later. For now, however, we must press on!

(7) Statement (c), 'All my future statements will be false'. Again, it is difficult to believe that a person could be so certain that he will lie on every occasion in the future. Yet Epimenides may make just one more false statement and then commit suicide, or be run over by a chariot, rendering statement (c) conceivably true, yet without the paradox, since it is referring to future statements, not the present statement. However, this idea of predetermining the future itself needs further discussion and clarification and will have a strong bearing on the solution of the present paradox and that of others in this volume.

(8) Statements (a) and (c), then, are found to be potentially true components of the larger statement (a) (b) (c). That is to say, the statement, 'Every statement I make is a lie' has been found in the cases of (a) and (c) to be at least potentially true, even if not very probable. As far as they are concerned, therefore, there is no paradox, because we have yet to determine the value of (b).

(9) The sticking point, as we have seen, is (b), 'This statement is false'. This is indeed paradoxical, since it is self-referential and not concerned with past or future. It cannot be wriggled out of. There is no escape route. It has to be faced.

'This statement is false' is the version of the Liar paradox that I shall be utilizing, and of course I am assuming it to be self-referential rather than referring to some other statement that is external to itself. Other versions, such as 'I am lying' or 'This is a lie' are second best, in my opinion, because they divert some attention away from the statement itself towards a consideration of what a person may or may not be thinking. All statements or propositions have a human origin, even if created randomly by computer or other means, but this human input is too prominent and intrusive in these versions. A third version, 'This sentence is false', is too sloppily constructed, since a sentence is a collection of words only and does not involve itself in such issues. A sentence is but the *vehicle* for a proposition, not the proposition itself. 'This is false' I similarly reject. This *what*? This *sentence*? This *word*?

So, 'This statement is false' seems to me one of the purest versions, and it will become clear later why I do not favour using 'This proposition is false'. 'This statement is false' is a sentence whose structure takes the form of a proposition. Propositions always have an inbuilt claim to factual status. They assert of themselves that they are true. Or at least, that is the implicit convention that we accept in our usage of them. By employing such verbs as *am, is, are, was, were*, propositions take on an air of authority. This is why the Liar paradox is so fiendishly effective in sending our heads into a giddy spin. It does not ask, 'Is this false?' which would leave our brains relatively unmolested, but goes straight in seemingly to challenge and contradict its own inherent claim to truth. Pictorial counterparts of this paradox, such as a snake swallowing its own tail, are often used as an aid in visualizing this idea of vicious circularity.

Vicious Circles and Belisha Beacons

There *is*, of course, a strong element of vicious circularity, since one conclusion (true) leads on to its opposite (false) and then back again, and so it carries on – ad infinitum, if we are crazy enough to allow it. However, 'circularity' could suggest a continuum, that there is no clean break between true and false, that the two gradually blend one into the other rather than being polar opposites. In reality, of course, what we *do* experience is something quite different: 'true' and 'false' alternately flash on and off like Belisha beacons, the lights that appear on our roads at zebra crossings. Again, though, the analogy is not perfect, since we should not equate 'true' with the positive of light and 'false' with the negative of light's absence. Opposites though true and false may be, they nevertheless enjoy equal status as far as their reflection of facts is concerned. If 'The door is open' is found to be true, we gain no greater degree of knowledge than if we discover it to be false – an open door is not positive and a closed door negative. Perhaps, then, our Belisha beacons should flash, not on and off, but from one colour to another, so that both truth and falsity are regarded as positive in regard to the knowledge they accord us; yet, the problem with this is that the two colours are now no longer seen as opposites. With this in mind, we shall return to the 'Belisha beacon' phenomenon later on in order to consider what may be the cause of it. And yet, all of this vicious circularity and flashing on and off do not really occur at all, as we shall come to see …

Two Very Important Laws of Logic

A proposition is the content of a sentence that affirms or denies something and is capable of being true or false. It comprises a subject and a predicate. For example, in the proposition 'The door is open', the subject is the door and the predicate is what is claimed regarding the door, i.e. that it is open. By observing the particular door to which the proposition is referring it should be possible to determine whether it is open or closed, and therefore whether the proposition is true or false.

The law of excluded middle states that a proposition must be either true or false and that there cannot be anything in between. One or the other. Either or. This or that.

The law of non-contradiction states that a proposition cannot be both true *and* false, as this would result in impermissible and illogical contradiction.

So, for example, with the statement 'The light is on', either the light is on or it is not. If it is on, then the statement is true. If it is not on, then the statement is false. There can be nothing in-between these two states. Even if the light works on a dimmer switch and you turn the switch only part of the way to produce only a very dim light, the light is nevertheless on and so the statement is true. Nor can the same light ever be on and off at the very same time. It cannot be both.

Therefore, the difficulty we have with the Liar paradox is that it must be either true or false in order to satisfy the law of excluded middle; yet if this law *is* to be satisfied it immediately breaks the law of non-contradiction. That is to say, if we declare it to be true, this entails that we simultaneously declare it to be false, and vice versa. Our task, therefore, is to work out what is going on – and what is going wrong – here. If these two laws are sound, then there must be something wrong with the statement that contains the Liar paradox, mustn't there? Or perhaps our notion of what constitutes truth and falsity is in need of revision? Something has to give. Will it be the two laws – found to be applicable in all cases but one? Or will it be the paradox – found to contradict not *these* laws, but others which perhaps take precedence and which as yet have lain undiscovered? In other words, has some *prior* malfunction brought the Liar sentence into direct conflict with these two laws of logic, so that this paradox only *appears* to be violating or negating them?

Previous Attempts to Solve the Liar Paradox

The Liar has been dubbed a semantic paradox and every attempt at solving it that I have encountered has focused largely on the nature of truth and falsity or has introduced the idea of a hierarchy of language, and so on. While these approaches may to some extent be understandable, I do not believe they have been particularly illuminating or convincing. If we are to concentrate almost exclusively on language and logic we may very easily overlook other factors that are at work in this paradox, and this could be the reason why for over two and a half thousand years it has resisted all attempts at a solution.

My own experience is that an explanation will also involve

elements such as, for example, sequence, consciousness, time, and that therefore, of necessity, we must overstep any artificially imposed boundaries and venture a little into the realm of scientific enquiry. But first, if we are to unlock the secrets of the Liar paradox, we need to contemplate a few basics – and grapple with language!

Human Origins

Imagine a piece of card with a proposition written on it, which lies in a field. The insects, the birds, the animals that fly past or walk by may well see the words that are written on the card, but they do not recognize them for what they are, let alone that they form something called a sentence which in turn contains a proposition which must be either true or false. Only when a human being comes along who has been taught that these strange marks are actually symbols for letters which form words and so on, can the sentence then take the form of a proposition. We could argue similarly for a spoken proposition. A proposition is an entirely human construct and it is only in the *human* mind, or consciousness, that a proposition exists, nowhere else. As was stated earlier, even if a proposition is randomly generated by computer or some other method, its origin is human and the recognition and understanding of it will be brought about solely by a human being.

Authority of a Proposition

We have suggested that propositions seem to possess an inherent authority, in that they assert something to be factual or true. They seem to throw out a challenge to us – 'they' know something that we perhaps do not. Furthermore, a proposition written on a piece of card that we find lying in the middle of nowhere appears equally as powerful as one spoken to us by a human being. Yet this is hardly surprising, since propositions apparently are the repositories of all the world's knowledge: 'The Earth is round'; 'Water boils at 100 degrees Celsius at sea level', etc. However, propositions apparently are also bearers of all the world's falsehoods: 'The moon is made of cheese'; 'The sun orbits Earth', etc.

Neutrality

We have given the definition of a proposition as, 'The content of a sentence that affirms or denies something and is capable of being true or false', and this definition is quite adequate for our purposes here. There can be a tendency to believe that the truth or falsity of a proposition is latent or hidden within it in some way and that it merely takes a little bit of effort on our part in order to expose which of the two it really is. This is because convention has bestowed upon the proposition a built-in bias. Once a proposition has been subjected to the verification process and found to be factual or non-factual, we may tend to regard that proposition as having all along sneakily concealed from us the reality that it was true or false, as if it possessed a consciousness, a power, or a life of its own. Yet I will argue that propositions always remain neutral as far as their truth-value is concerned, otherwise they cease to be propositions and become something else.

Imagine, if you will, a man dressed from top to toe in grey – grey for neutral – and we shall say that he represents a proposition. However, he comes across to us as being rather self-confident or cocky, as if he really does know whether or not what he is asserting is indeed factual. We observe that he is wearing a grey (!) zip-up jacket, and occasionally he fiddles with the zip, as if about to undo the jacket and reveal his real self. His real self, of course, will be represented by a bright green tee-shirt which indicates that he has been a true proposition all along, (so why did we doubt him!), or a vivid red tee-shirt which discloses that he had been fooling us all the time, for he is a false proposition (and how he enjoyed stringing us along!).

Yet our man in grey never does unzip his jacket. Never. He does not wear a coloured tee-shirt beneath his outerwear. There is nothing hidden. Were we at all able to unzip his jacket, we would discover him to have yet another layer of grey. Nevertheless, green and red tee-shirts will eventually come to disturb our grey man, as we shall explain later.

Questions and Propositions

Verbs such as *am*, *is*, *are*, *was*, *were*, seem to afford propositions their assertive air of authority. Yet this is only due to their position within a sentence, and it is only usage and custom which grant propositions their special privileges. We use propositions constantly in our day to day lives as a means of communication and in the transmission of knowledge and information. Reporting what you have done, what so-and-so said, what your holiday plans are, etc., all entail the use of propositions, of sentences which assert something to be factual, true. By and large we do not question these statements, particularly when they are uttered by people whom we trust, such as family, friends and colleagues. Nor should we, since the vast majority of such statements made by them *will* be honest and truthful and it is proper that we should accept them unhesitatingly. However, in reality, the proposition, 'The door is open', has no greater power than the question, 'Is the door open?' The latter assumes no claim to authority, has no built-in bias: it merely asks, and leaves the answer for us to determine. Were we to place a question mark at the end of the proposition we would leave its sentence structure intact, yet radically alter its status: 'The door is open?' seems now to be a question that is asked, perhaps, in response to someone stating 'The door is open', or just as an unorthodox way of asking, 'Is the door open?'

Whatever it may be, it is nothing other than the proposition in a different guise, and in reality this is exactly how we should view all propositions at all times: with a question mark at their rear. Propositions are not inherently true or false. They are neutral. If they have the capacity to be true *or* false then they *must* be neutral. Only when we do something about them do we encounter these true or false values, in much the same way that we might find an answer to a question.

'Will the crocodile become extinct in the year 2074?'
'The crocodile will become extinct in the year 2074.'

These two sentences were created within the last two minutes. Why crocodiles? I don't know – perhaps because a nasty crocodile rears its ugly head later on in this book. Why the year 2074? I don't know that, either. The first sentence is totally innocent, yet it seems to raise a possibility that didn't exist previously. Is there a terrible disease lurking out there somewhere that is about to wipe out these reptiles? Is there a rogue asteroid on its way to our planet that is destined even now to wipe out most living things that year? The second sentence – the proposition – seems to go even further, to have some predictive power or insider knowledge – but only if we let it. The human imagination is responsible for these flights of fancy, yet we attribute many of its aerobatics to the proposition itself. It couldn't possibly be true or false, since we have not yet reached the year 2074. Neither the question nor the proposition are wearing coloured tee-shirts. They are both dressed entirely in entirely-neutral grey.

Yet at midnight on 31st December, 2074, the above proposition will become false. Or perhaps at some point earlier in the year it will become true. What is going on here?

15

Does a proposition change from being neutral to being either true or false after all? Is there some mysterious process that kicks in at some point to undermine everything we have just been arguing? Or is something else occurring that we have yet to discover?

No, I haven't forgotten about the Liar paradox. All of this is leading us nearer to it. In a little while I shall be challenging and revising the commonly held views regarding propositions being either true or false, as I have begun to do above, but before I do I shall be sticking with the status quo in order to address some other basic concerns regarding the proposition.

Logical Admissibility

I accept the two-valued system of logic. That is to say, I believe that a proposition must become either true or false, with nothing in between. Some philosophers have suggested that there should indeed be a third category, for those propositions that are nonsensical. But in order to say that a sentence is nonsensical you need to have hard and fast rules which will dictate when a proposition does not come up to standard. When a proposition is rejected under these conditions I would prefer to say that it is a *neutral statement* rather than a nonsensical one. To say that a sentence is nonsense is too vague, too woolly, giving no indication of why it has failed as a proposition, and also contains a hint of emotion in the rejection – impatience, perhaps!

So, having stated that I believe in a two-valued system of logic, yet also recognize that some propositions are logically inadmissible, am I contradicting myself, since there now seem to be three alternatives in play? The answer is No, for reasons that I shall try to make clear. To my mind, there is always a third option – that a statement is logically inadmissible as a proposition if a clean and unambiguous true or false value cannot be obtained for it, either actually or potentially. A statement can only qualify as a genuine proposition if it is capable of being either wholly true or wholly false. There can be no compromises.

For example, if I state, 'There are more than twenty words on page 48 of this book', you will be able to test this proposition and determine if it is true or false. But if I state, 'There are more than twenty words on page 448 of this book', you certainly cannot respond with a 'true', since there aren't anywhere near that number of pages in this book. However, nor can you respond with a 'false', since that would imply that you have discovered fewer than twenty words on page 448. Because there is no such page – because the *subject* of the statement is missing – the only proper response that we can give to the statement is that it is inadmissible as a proposition. It remains a statement, not a proposition, since it has not met all the criteria necessary for such a sentence to be designated a proposition. Thus, a statement that has the capacity to be declared only and solely true or false following some verification procedure such as a test, experiment, observation, is worthy to be elevated to the rank of proposition, but if such is impossible, for whatever reason, then the sentence fails to step up to the required mark and remains a lowly statement, and a pointless one at that. However, there are those who do not take this view, who believe that because a statement such as the one above cannot possibly be true, then it cannot be declared anything other than false. I shall explain further why I make a distinction between the two.

Let us take another statement.

'At this very moment, the front door of Rose Cottage is open.'

Now, let us assume you are just around the corner and can take a peek at Rose Cottage. But, to make it a little bit easier for you and to save your legs, turn to the next page of this book, where you will find Rose Cottage ready and waiting for you. Let's pretend this is the real thing.

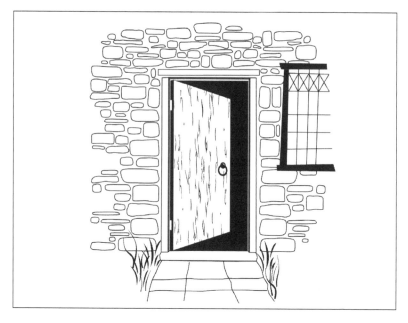

3. Front door of Rose Cottage (a)

If you have done that, you can with certainty say that the above proposition is either true or false. But now I would like to trouble you again, if I may. It is a couple of hours later and you have returned to the same corner (what an exciting life you lead!), when your friend Jack repeats the very same statement you responded to earlier in the day. However, friend Emily states exactly the opposite. Neither of them has looked at the cottage before making their statement, so what you have just heard is as follows.

> Jack: 'At this very moment, the front door of Rose Cottage is open.'
> Emily: 'At this very moment, the front door of Rose Cottage is closed.'

You have already looked at Rose Cottage once, and that is probably more than enough for one day, thank you very much; but as pointless as the statements may appear to be, your curiosity, your need to know, will probably overwhelm you and you will be unable to resist taking another little peek. Go on, you only have to go the next page.

Thank you. You have now witnessed the fact that the lovely Rose Cottage is missing its front door and this is not what you expected to see at all. Has it been stolen? Is it being repaired? Painted? Varnished? Whatever the reason for its absence, you now have to report back to Jack and Emily, responding 'true' or 'false' to their statements. First Jack. No cheating – just because the doorway of Rose Cottage allows entry, you cannot say 'true', since it is the *door* that is allegedly open, *not* the doorway. There is no door to be open. In which case, are you going to reply 'false'? If you do, Jack will automatically think that, since it is false that the front door is open, therefore the door must be closed. But that isn't so, is it?

What of Emily, then? You certainly cannot say 'true', for obvious reasons, but if you say 'false' she will quite understandably infer from this that the door must be open. Yet there is no door. It is no good saying to both Jack and Emily, 'False, because there is no front door'. When verifying a proposition, it should not need to be qualified – 'true' or 'false' *only* is all that is required. One or the other. Either or. This or that. Jack and Emily's statements are polar opposites and if neither of them can be true then neither of them can be false. If both are declared false then in effect we are saying that the door is both open and closed. This is impossible. It violates the law of non-contradiction. But forget about this law – just show me a door that can be simultaneously open and closed when in place and I shall pay you handsomely for it (for the door, that is, not just for showing me it).

The whole purpose of a proposition, its *raison d'etre*, is to act as a kind of servant for the human consciousness: it does a job of work for us. But unless it is structured properly it will be like some kind of machine that is missing one or other of its component parts and it will shudder and judder to a halt. If a car is lacking its

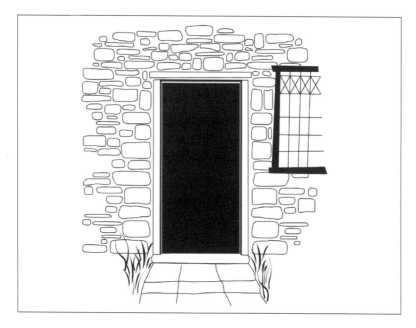

4. Front door of Rose Cottage (b)

gearbox or its engine or its wheels, then it is not fully entitled to be called a car, since it is not fully functional. Similarly, if a cottage is lacking its front door and a proposition fails to reflect this fact when supposedly transmitting information regarding it, then it is not fully functioning as a proposition. It may well be structurally sound as a sentence, with a word or words that act as a subject (the door) and others that acts as a predicate (is open/is closed), but a proposition is not meant to be just a string of words that looks good, a thing in and of itself, self-indulgent and standing aloof from the rest of the world; rather, it has a practical purpose to its seemingly abstract life. A proposition is supposed to provide us with an opportunity to gain knowledge, but if it is deficient in one of its component parts then it is living under false pretences and must be demoted to the ranks, i.e. be declared a neutral statement, since it is a failed proposition.

If we were right to say that the two statements of Jack and Emily are false, because there is no door to be either open or closed, then we would be equally justified in taking a similar approach in other circumstances. For instance, if we take Jack's statement, that the door is open, and discover that there is a door but it is closed, we could come back with the response that the statement, though false, is also partially true, because at least there *is* a door. In other words, we are taking our eye off the ball and rewarding the proposition with a 'true', when all along there very well *should* be a door. This simply will not do. A proposition is either wholly, fully, completely true or false or it is not a proposition. There can be no compromises.

Sentences are not true or false. Rather, it is what is being asserted of something else, what is being predicated of a subject, through the medium of a sentence, that is true or false, not the sentence as a whole. A sentence is merely a vehicle for a proposition: its words and form convey it. So, in this instance, the status of the door – open or closed – is what is true or false, *not* the sentence as a whole. The existence of the door in the real, objective world should be a given, unquestionable, and should not exist merely in the twilight world of the subjective mind. The abstract should have its counterpart in the concrete. That is what a proposition is all about.

For the sake of further clarity, I shall extend the analogy given above regarding the car. It will not be perfect – analogies seldom are – but hopefully it will make things a little plainer for us, as using sentences to talk about sentences can become a little bit claustrophobic after a while.

So, let us liken a proposition to a car. Every proposition/car looks different to all others, yet each has a gearbox, engine, wheels, and so on and is perfectly formed, otherwise it will not function as it should. Each car's sole purpose is to drive along a straight, featureless road into the far distance that no one can make out, until it reaches a white line that is painted across the width of the road. As soon as the car crosses this line it will instantaneously veer to the left or to the right on a road which miraculously appears out of nowhere. This road, left or right, cannot be seen in advance of *crossing* the line as it simply does not exist yet. The type of car, in combination with the white line, triggers a left or right turn. Painted on the roof, bonnet and sides of each car, in large letters, is the statement 'This car turns left' or 'This car turns right', but the trouble is no one can be sure if this statement reflects reality. You examine a 'left' car closely and observe that it resembles another car that you know from experience was a left-turner, so you are able to make an educated guess, but in reality you can never really know unless you ride in the car.

A friend of yours says that she has made the journey in that particular car and it definitely does turn to the left. Your friend is trustworthy and in all other respects generally reliable, so you are inclined to believe her. But at the next moment a passer-by, who notices you scrutinising the car and pondering over it, 'helpfully' shouts, 'Turns to the right, mate, every time.' Now you really are confused. Only one thing for it – you must take the car for a spin yourself. True knowledge can only come from personal experience, you think to yourself. So you hop in and off you go. You may hop back out again at any time before you reach the white line, but once you cross it your perception of the car and its statement will be changed forever. So, you cross the white line and now you know whether the statement is true or false. You return the car to its original starting point and tell others who look it over what the facts are regarding it. But they are in exactly the same predicament as you were earlier on: they can never really know the truth of the matter unless they, too, take the car down the road and cross the white line.

But remember, the only thing that is true or false is whether the car turns to the left or to the right. Nothing else. The statement on the car cannot be false due to a lack of gearbox or engine or wheels or any other component. The statement refers to the direction in which the car turns, not to the car itself. If the car is deficient in its parts then it is the car-maker's job to either scrap it as unroadworthy ('There is no front door at Rose Cottage, so the statement is inadmissible'), or rebuild it ('At this very moment, the front door of Rose Cottage is missing'). What would happen if you turned the corner to find that, not just the door, but Rose Cottage itself was missing, that it did not exist? Do the two statements now seem *even more* false or *even more* inadmissible – if such is possible (I do not believe it is!)? Perhaps the sentences are now degenerating into nonsense – and it is this nonsense that I prefer to call inadmissible. Lacking a whole cottage or a little door, it does not matter which.

Should a failed proposition be deemed inadmissible? After all, the *form* of each of the sentences is acceptable: they have a subject (the door) and a predicate (is open/is closed). But again, it must be stressed that it is the *content* that is the all-important element of a proposition. The sentence alone, perfectly *formed* in its construction as it may be, exists within the subjective mind as a statement, but unless the subject and predicate have a correlation with the objective, external world it cannot qualify as a proposition. As an idea in your mind, fine, nothing wrong with that – except that this is often the realm of fiction. Have this idea reflect what is going on in the real world and we are now dealing with fact. This is the whole purpose of a proposition.

So, should a failed proposition be deemed exactly that, a *failed proposition*, rather than an *inadmissible statement*? Perhaps. Alternatively, we could dub it a *pseudo-proposition*. But if a would-be proposition is not doing its proper job, if its subject is not as it is presented and implied within the sentence, or its predicate does not exist within the bounds of possibility, then it is an imposter and should be driven out of town. There are certain expectations that we have of propositions, certain rules that we demand they should adhere to and certain tasks that they should perform; and to my mind statements which do not meet such expectations are illegitimate. Therefore, I shall continue to describe such sentences as *inadmissible statements*, though others may prefer to term them something else.

Whatever we may prefer to call them, they are certainly *neutral* as far as their truth-value is concerned. They are neither true nor false. And if they are not propositions then we need have no concerns regarding a potential violation of the law of excluded middle. While a proposition may inhabit the sphere of neutrality prior to testing, it always possesses the capability to become either true or false. The failed proposition or inadmissible statement that we have been discussing possesses no such capability and is doomed to eternal neutrality.

Context

Let us take the proposition, 'The door is open'. In and of itself this is inadequate. We need to ask, 'Which door?' and 'The door is open on which date and at what particular time?' We need to know the *context* when considering propositions such as these, which are open to more than one interpretation, otherwise they do not make full sense nor permit of full verification.

Employing such care as this will have the additional benefit of disallowing a proposition to be true at one moment and false the next. For example, if you refer to a particular set of traffic lights and state, 'The lights are at red', this will be true at one moment and false shortly after, then back to true again, only to be followed by false, and so on. Stipulate the precise time as well as the precise place and such oscillation will be eliminated. These precautions amount to no more than common sense. Of course, the situation does not always require us to be explicit in every detail in regard to what we are asserting; this is fine, as long as all parties are clear as to the what and the where and the when.

Some Rules for An Admissible Proposition

1. The subject term must have a counterpart in the real world, when such is presented and implied within the statement.
2. The predicate term must be in accord with what can be rationally asserted of the given subject. So, 'The carrot is sobbing' just will not do. 'The cartoon carrot is sobbing' may well just pass muster.
3. The context, i.e. location in time and space, must be specified or in some way indicated. We need What? Where? When?
4. Any ambiguities in 1, 2, 3, or in any other element of the sentence, must be removed by reformulating the proposition, such that all interested parties are in agreement.
5. The proposition, when tested, must be capable of yielding an *unqualified* 'true' or 'false' response.

Verification Statements

Let us take again the proposition, 'The door is open', and let us call the person who makes this statement the *stater*. If the stater is looking or pointing at the door in question at the very moment that he makes the statement, and the door is open, then from his perspective one of two things could be happening.

1. The stater made the statement a split second *before* visually and mentally determining whether or not the door was in fact open, so for him the statement was a proposition, since it was still 'capable of being true or false'.
2. The stater made the statement a split second *after* visually and mentally determining that the door was open, so for him the statement he makes cannot be a proposition, since it is not 'capable of being true or false'. He has issued what to him is a

statement of fact. He has stated the truth. Because the stater *knows* the status of the door (open or closed) and the statement derives from this knowledge, I shall call this kind of sentence a *verification statement*, because the door's status has been verified. Let us also make it plain that in using the word 'verify' and its derivatives I intend it to mean determine the truth *or* falsity of a proposition and not just confirm its truth.

However, if the stater says, 'The door is open', knowing full well that the door is closed, the statement he makes is, once again, a verification statement, not a proposition, though obviously a verification statement of a very different type.

So, if you *do not* know the status of something in regard to its truth or falsity, your statement is a proposition; if you *do* know, it is a verification statement.

There are, however, two types of verification statement, as we have seen: one of them expresses a fact and the other expresses a falsehood. We might, therefore, designate them a *true verification statement* and a *false verification statement*. Something of a mouthful, perhaps, yet they do help us to distinguish between these different types of statement, and will serve as helpful steps in understanding and solving the Liar paradox. We could, perhaps, abbreviate them to *tvs* and *fvs* for convenience's sake, but it is easy to get bogged down by too many acronyms and to forget what they mean.

The stater knows whether his sentence, 'The door is open', is a proposition or a verification statement (fact or falsehood), but everyone else, at least initially, is ignorant of these distinctions. From their perspective, 'The door is open' is *always* a proposition, it is *always* a statement in need of verification. This is because we cannot read another person's mind (we shall omit the possibility of telepathy, the reading of body language and similar considerations from our discussion!) and always need to determine truth or falsity independently of other people. In other words, we need to do it for ourselves. 'True' and 'false' are properties of the human consciousness, not properties of a sentence.

For example, if we are looking at an open door at which the stater points and then says, 'The door is open', even though we can agree with him that what he has just stated is a fact and therefore the truth, we nevertheless still had to test his statement before we could offer our assent. It may take only a fraction of a second, yet we shall either refresh our perception of the door *or* speedily consult our memory of having just a second ago looked at the door. This type of process *must always* take place before we can say that a statement is either true or false. If the door had been closed when the stater said 'The door is open', a similar process would have been undertaken in order for us to say that the statement is non-factual and therefore false. Therefore, to everyone other than the stater, a statement that he makes which purports to be factual, initially at least will always be a proposition.

Let us take a simple mathematical equation, which is really just another type of proposition, and see if the same procedure takes place.

$$3 + 3 = 6$$

This is obviously true. How easy is that! But did we add 3 and 3 to make 6 before we agreed that this equation was correct, true? Or did we rapidly access our memory, without really thinking about it, and immediately agree that $3 + 3 = 6$ because we are just so familiar with this little sum that we no longer need to do the calculation? How about the following, then?

$$1 + 2 + 3 + 4 = 10$$

Did this sum take a little longer this time? Calculation or memory? Try this one.

$$1.26 + 2.75 + 3.14 + 2.85 = 10$$

Longer again? Calculation only? Is the equation correct? If this sum became very familiar to us, eventually we would have no need to do the calculation, but would rely on our memory of *having at one time* done the adding up.

So, I hope you will agree that, between a proposition and a true/false response to it, there will – and must always – be some intervening stage of verification.

Verification Procedure

	Test	
	Experiment	
Proposition	Observation	True/False
	Calculation	
	Memory	
	Logical Analysis	
	Etc.	

5. Verification Procedure

Indeed, before a person can even respond to a proposition with a 'true' or 'false', he first of all has to recognize the proposition *as* a proposition. That is to say, the human consciousness, the mind, must engage with the spoken or written sentence and recognize it as being more than just a collection of sounds, or squiggles on a piece of paper. Quite a few things need to go on within the consciousness before we can ever utter an affirmative or a negative, and we shall explore more of them soon.

It is important we agree that a proposition must submit to a verification procedure (some types of which are listed above) before a true or false value can be assigned to it. Without such agreement there could never be for you an acceptable solution to the Liar paradox that I could offer. However, I feel sure that, upon reflection, you will concur that such a process does, in fact, always take place as part of the natural scheme of things and that this is not an artificial or contrived notion. It is nature, psychology, reality – call it what you will.

Truth and falsity are designations that belong in a proposition's logical future, but that future will only occur when a proposition is made to go through a transitional stage in which it is tested in one form or another. From that test will emerge a knowledge or certainty regarding whether the assertion made by the sentence – which we call a proposition – is factual or non-factual and consequently true or false.

Solving the Liar Paradox

I shall be attacking the Liar paradox on three major fronts. Firstly, I shall be exposing the paradox's violation of the logical future, a crime that I have dubbed *malsequence*. Secondly, I shall be arguing that the paradox is locked in a condition of immobility, or stasis, and never actually reaches the level of contradiction, of paradox, at all. Thirdly, I shall be arguing that even if the level of paradox *could* be reached, it would be neutrality that we experience, not contradiction.

Malsequence

One of the Olympic athletes to whom I introduced you at the very beginning was called Liar Paradox. You may recall that she insisted she had won the next day's 100 metres final and already had the gold medal in her possession to prove it. Well, of course, such a feat is impossible. No one, as far as we know, is able to travel into a future that does not yet exist and then return to the present with an object removed from that future. This athlete's claim is absurd.

I shall be arguing here that the Liar paradox is guilty of precisely the same type of offence – that it is travelling into the future, both logical and temporal, and bringing back from that future, into the present, a mental event that does not yet exist. This, again, is impossible and absurd.

When I speak of the logical future I mean that there are certain things which exist in a certain order, which occupy a specific place in a logical sequence, a sequence which cannot be interfered with or offended against. If we count from 1 to 10, for example, we know exactly what to expect.

$$1\ 2\ 3\ 4\ 5\ 6\ 7\ 8\ 9\ 10$$

However, if we were to encounter the following sequence, we would immediately recognize that a grave logical error had occurred.

$$1\ 2\ 3\ 4\ 7\ 5\ 6\ 8\ 9\ 10$$

I think we would all readily agree that the number 7 (and therefore also 5 and 6) has been displaced from its regular and *logical* place, that there is a serious fault here. The number 7 cannot precede the numbers 5 and 6; the number 7 can only be reached and achieved *subsequent* to the place it currently occupies. For this reason, as stated, I am calling this phenomenon, in which a transgression of the logical or natural order has occurred, *malsequence*. Something which belongs in, and to, the logical future has been installed in an earlier position – illegitimately. This is a wrong, bad, faulty, defective sequence – hence *mal*sequence.

The number sequence 1 2 3 4 7 5 6 8 9 10 is suffering from malsequence. Before we can arrive at 7 there need to be some intervening steps, namely 5 and 6. They are *necessary*, not optional, and necessary both in a logical and a mathematically practical sense.

When we consider the sentence, 'This statement is false', the 'false' component of the sentence has been introduced from the logical future. A 'false' or 'true' conclusion cannot be applied to a proposition until that proposition has been in some way verified, put to the test.

But not only has the logical future been violated, the temporal future equally has been wronged, because 'true' and 'false' can only be reached logically by also traversing a period of time: to test a proposition and arrive at a conclusion regarding it will involve some degree of temporal expenditure. So, the malsequence that has taken place in the Liar paradox is both logical and temporal, in the same way that a planted apple pip which produces an apple without any intervening tree or blossom has offended the logical and temporal (and natural!) order. Pip → tree → blossom → apple; not pip → apple. Proposition → test → knowledge → true or false; not proposition → true or false. You cannot skip the tree; you cannot skip the test.

The Liar paradox is akin to a mini time machine. Off it goes, hurtling into the not-yet-existent future, grabbing a trophy, and then zooming back with it before anyone has even noticed, confusing and confounding us thereby.

The Life-Cycle of a Proposition

We need to make this idea, this claim, more explicit and comprehensible, and we can do this simply by observing the procedures and steps that occur during the life-cycle of a proposition. In order to clarify it still further, I shall then express it schematically.

Let us take our familiar friend, 'The door is open', and assume that context has been established, all ambiguity removed, and that this is indeed a proposition because it is capable of being declared true or false. Here, then, are the steps that are necessary for it to undergo.

1. The statement is such that it achieves the status of a proposition, i.e. *there is* a functioning door. The proposition is held in the consciousness until the act of verification takes place.

2. As soon as a test, experiment – or in this case, an observation – is performed, we have, in consciousness, encountered the *verification boundary*, the point at which a proposition is matched or compared with reality and a value for it obtained: true or false. The verification boundary is equivalent to the tape broken by an athlete in a race. In our earlier analogy of the cars, it is the white line painted across the width of the road. The boundary is the interface – the meeting point – between the proposition and the reality it claims to represent. It is the clear-cut line between the unknowing and the knowing. It is totally neutral. I shall have more to say about it in due course, and this discussion will involve the Gödel sentence.

3. The test successfully completed, the boundary crossed, we instantly experience a realization in consciousness, a moment of *knowing* in regard to the proposition. That is to say, we now *personally* see that the door is open or closed; or *personally* observe that the thermometer indicates 100° Celsius at the very instant that the water boils at sea-level. This instant of *knowing* I shall call the *verification moment*. We now realize that, Yes the door *is* open, or No, the door *is not* open, or Yes, water *does* boil at 100° Celsius at sea-level.

4. Mentally, we now progress to the *verification response*, whereby a 'true' or 'false' value is assigned to, or conferred upon, the proposition. It is at this point that the proposition undergoes a metamorphosis in our consciousness due to our personal

encounter with it and the reality it allegedly represents. Remember the man dressed entirely in neutral grey? We might say that, in conferring true or false status upon the proposition, we are now mentally clothing the man in a green or red tee-shirt which conceals the neutral grey beneath and marks him out for all time as being true or false. But this action exists only in *our* consciousness, no one else's. Unless you have *personally* tested the proposition, the man will forever be attired in neutral grey and there will be no metamorphosis, no transmutation. In our eyes, *there is no longer a proposition*: for us, there is in its place only a *fact* or a *falsehood* – the proposition has disappeared! Pre-verification, 'The door is open' was something of a mystery to us: we did not know one way or the other whether it was true or false. Post-verification, we now have certainty, and the exact same statement, 'The door is open', has entirely lost its mystery and become either a fact or a falsehood. This loss of mystery has led to the statement completely changing its character and for us, *eternally*, it can never again be a proposition. To anyone else who has not crossed the verification boundary, however, 'The door is open' will *eternally* remain a proposition. The very same statement, therefore, may take on very different characteristics, depending on whether a person considers it from a pre-verification or a post-verification perspective, and so we might say that there is an element of relativity involved.

5. If this 'true' or 'false' realization is now converted into words – verbal, written or both – then this expression becomes what I earlier termed a *verification statement*. It is the equivalent of feedback. We said that this type of statement could take either of two forms: true or false. Let us suppose that the proposition, 'The door is open', has been found by me to be true. I now say to you that the proposition is true, yet you have not been to observe the door as I have. You may well take my word on this because you trust me, but you can never really be sure whether the proposition is true or not without

testing it for yourself, *personally*. From my position of privilege, I know whether my verification statement is the truth or a lie, but you do not. From your perspective, therefore, my verification statement is, again, nothing more than a proposition. You may invest it with more credibility than it has in reality because of your trust in me, yet your trust may be entirely misplaced. If I say, 'Honestly, it's true', or 'I swear to you, it's true', or 'As God is my witness, and on the lives of all my family, it's true', it does not matter one jot. It may all be a lie. Remember the race commentator who is the spitting image of one of the athletes? Why not visit her again to refresh your memory? Her name is Verification Statement.

Proposition	Verification Boundary	Verification Moment	Verification Response	Verification Statement
Examples:	Test Experiment			(Feedback)
The door is open 2+3=7	**Observation**	The door *is* open. PROPOSITION DISAPPEARS. NOW A FACT.	True	Proposition is true (but may state that it is false)
	Calculation	$2+3=5$ PROPOSITION DISAPPEARS. NOW A FALSEHOOD.	False	Equation is false (but may state that it is true)
	Memory etc.			

6. The life-cycle of a proposition

It can be appreciated from the above diagram, and the earlier discussion, that the polar opposites, true and false, are states of consciousness, not properties of propositions. Therefore, for a (so-called) proposition to have incorporated within its structure a predicate of 'true' or 'false' is to commit a fundamental error. Both logically and temporally, such states do not yet exist in respect of the proposition. Remember: pip → tree → blossom → apple; not pip → apple. Similarly: proposition → test → knowledge → true/false; not proposition → true/false. 'This statement is true' and 'This statement is false' are both crossing the verification boundary illegitimately, capturing a *mental state, condition, realization* (call it what we will, it is a property of consciousness) and then crossing back over the boundary line to display the prize in the present.

'This statement is ...' looks fine and dandy so far, and would be a perfectly good proposition if it ended as '... composed of words', or ' ... self-referential', or as something similar; but instead it now sneaks over the border, kidnaps a verification statement, smuggles its contraband back over the border and introduces it into its construction as if everything is perfectly alright. It is not alright. Logically and practically, this cannot legitimately be done. *Propositions and verification statements occupy opposite sides of the verification boundary, which neither of them can ever cross.* One of them is from the Land of the Unknowing while the other is from the Land of the Knowing. Easy to entwine the two in imagination and in a sentence, for sure, but impossible to do in practice, and this is one of the reasons why we experience huge problems with the Liar paradox. We cannot embed the future in the present – the future does not yet exist! The Liar paradox is, therefore, a *hybrid* sentence. It is not a proposition. It is a blending, a splicing together, of two different types of statement: a proposition and a verification statement. In real experience, however, these two, whilst very similar, do not in fact enjoy any interaction at all and can never be legitimately combined.

To make this point abundantly clear, think again about the

antics of the Olympic athlete named Liar Paradox. Miss Paradox has not yet run in tomorrow's 100 metres final and crossed the finishing line, so she cannot possibly be the gold medallist and therefore she cannot lawfully have the gold medal in her possession. Similarly, the Liar sentence has not yet crossed the verification boundary – it has not been tested in an appropriate way – so it cannot possibly have been pronounced false in advance of the event. A gross transgression of the logical and temporal future has occurred. This is *malsequence*. What should occur subsequently has 'occurred' forcibly several steps before it even could. I repeat: *this future does not yet exist; true and false are responses resulting from the verification process and are states which exist solely within the human consciousness, not within propositions.*

In the Liar paradox we see that the usual steps: proposition, verification and true/false response, have all been contracted into a single sentence. A diagram will hopefully make the matter easier to understand.

Proposition	Verification Boundary	Verification Moment	Verification Response	Verification Statement
THE LIAR **This** **statement** NOT A PROPOSITION – A HYBRID	NO TEST PERFORMED	NO REALIZATION EXPERIENCED	WITH NOTHING VERIFIED THERE CAN BE NO TRUE/FALSE RESPONSE	**is false** YET HERE IS A SPOKEN (OR WRITTEN) RESPONSE TO THE STATEMENT

7. Analysis of the Liar sentence

This is the order of a proposition's life-cycle: 1. proposition → 2. verification boundary → 3. verification moment → 4. verification response → 5. verification statement. With the Liar, however, stages 2, 3 and 4 have never been visited, and all we have is 1/5, that is, stages 1 and 5 spliced together.

I wish to make my point about the hybrid sentence crystal clear, if I possibly can. In order to attempt this I shall convert the Liar into its question equivalent, and then into its equation equivalent. In this way, I believe the absurdity of this type of statement will more readily manifest itself to us and thereby render the error of the Liar sentence more apparent.

The Liar as a Question

The type of question to which I shall convert the Liar is that which requires only an affirmative or negative response. 'The door is open' requires a response of True or False only. 'The door is open?' requires a response of Yes or No only. Yes is equivalent to True, No is equivalent to False.

So, recast as a question, the Liar sentence will change from 'This statement is false' to 'This question is No?' Hopefully, already this question is looking decidedly dodgy. Can we not immediately see that, herein, two very different sentences have been contracted into one, that we have a half-formed question spliced together with its possible answer? Is it not also immediately apparent that the means of arriving at the answer is totally absent? The question's 'verification moment' has been bypassed. *Malsequence* is strongly in evidence. The 'question' is nothing other than nonsense. If we rearrange the words of the 'question' into a more familiar form, we have 'Is this question No?' Does it fare any better in this new format? Should we really fiddle with it some more and express it as 'Is the answer to this question No?'? This latter formulation would seem to generate the expected contradiction:

'Is the answer to this question No?' If it is yes, it is no; and if it is no, it is yes.

And yet, when we chew the matter over, do we not see that by answering Yes or No in response to this question we are falling into the trap that it sets us, just as we do with the Liar? It *cannot* be Yes. It *cannot* be No. What we really need to ask is whether, 'Is the answer to this question No?' is a legitimate question in the first place? We are fooled by it into believing that it is legitimate, because the splicing together of its half-formed question and its possible answer is so convincing as to invite little scrutiny, because it *seems* like a regular question. But of course it is not a properly constructed question and it is empty of any real content. It is another hybrid, and therefore a straightforward Yes or No response to it is inappropriate. I should like to call this question-equivalent of the Liar the 'Q-Liar'.

The Liar as an Equation

There is no directly equivalent, self-referential equation, I think, and yet every equation appears automatically to refer to itself anyway. $1 + 1 = 3$ does not invite us to look outside into the wider world for a response to it, but simply to deal with the numbers and the symbols it places before us. So I believe the same principles will apply to equations as to statements and questions. Therefore, let us now take a look at some legitimate and illegitimate statements, questions and equations.

Legitimate Constructions	Illegitimate Constructions
The door is open	The door is true
This statement comprises five words	This statement is true
The door is open?	The door is yes?
This question comprises five words?	This question is yes?
3+3=6	3+3=correct

The door is closed	The door is false
This statement comprises six words	This statement is false
The door is closed?	The door is no?
This question comprises six words?	This question is no?
3+3=5	3+3=wrong

8. Legitimate and illegitimate constructions

'3 + 3 = wrong' is an equation equivalent of 'This statement is false', and it contains exactly the same type of malsequence from which the Liar suffers. It is another hybrid. I should like to call this the 'E-Liar'.

To my mind, the E-Liar demonstrates in a far more direct and powerful way the problems of the Liar sentence than can its question equivalent, the Q-Liar, because we have half an equation combined with a response to its absent sum. As indicated above, another equivalent would be, 'The door is false'. Well, a door cannot be false (just to be very clear: yes, there are such things as false doors, but we are here concerned with 'false' as a truth-value, not 'false' as in not a real door). Nor can 3 + 3 be wrong. In both cases *the predicate is missing* and something other – a response from the logical future – has taken its place and is disguised as a predicate.

It is plain for everyone to see that the constructions on the left in the above table all require a separate response to them, whereas the constructions on the right have their responses already built-in, as it were, but nevertheless seem to require yet another response, and in this respect they mirror the construction of the Liar paradox.

The Liar's Non-Identical Twin

'This statement is true', as seen above right, is the Liar's non-identical twin, and often goes by the name of the Truth-teller. It has enjoyed very little of the limelight so copiously bestowed upon its more illustrious sibling. This is because the Liar's twin does not generate contradiction, but, strangely, something akin to reinforcement. Let us take a look at it to see what is meant.

'This statement is true.'

If the statement is true, it is true; and if the statement is false, it is false. No contradiction here, for sure, and yet there is most definitely a peculiar puzzle that arises from it which, as with the Liar itself, needs to be addressed. Can a statement be doubly true? Can a statement be doubly false? Why should such 'doubleness' appear in the first place? Why isn't there just *one* 'true' or just *one* 'false' as there is with other statements?

But then again, with the Liar itself, though it is contradiction that is the main feature rather than reinforcement, there is still a 'doubleness' in evidence. We say, 'If it is true, it is false; and if it is false, it is true'. Both twins, then, engender a double truth-value response: true/true; false/false; true/false; false/true. What, exactly, is going on here?

(Of course, the Truth-teller as a question, the Q-Truth-teller, would look like this: 'Is the answer to this question Yes?' If it is yes, it is yes; if it is no, it is no. The Truth-teller as an equation, the E-Truth-teller, would be: $3 + 3 =$ correct.)

The Moment of Proof

A proposition gives us two jobs of work to do. For example, with 'The door is open', first of all we do not know if the door really is open, and secondly we do not know if the proposition is true or false. Let us suppose that we test the proposition: now we know that the door is open or is not open, *and* now we know that the proposition is either true or false.

It will be agreed, I am sure, that knowledge regarding the status of the door (open or not open) is of primary concern, while knowledge regarding the status of the proposition (true or false) is of secondary concern. A proposition, then, has two types of content: explicit, or external, which is an assertion regarding a state of affairs somewhere 'out there' ('The door is open'); and implicit, or internal, which is an assertion regarding the proposition's own truth-value ('I am a true statement' is what *every* proposition seems to imply of itself). I should like to call the external element of a proposition its *primary content* and the internal element of a proposition its *secondary content.* When we come to successfully test a proposition, we shall now have *primary knowledge* and *secondary knowledge.* That is to say, in the case of 'The door is open', I now *know* whether or not the door is open (primary knowledge) and I additionally *know* that the proposition is either true or false (secondary knowledge). Primary content has been transformed into primary knowledge and secondary content has been transformed into secondary knowledge.

Recalling what has been said in regard to malsequence, we can confidently state that primary knowledge must always precede secondary knowledge: we cannot, for example, know that 'The door is open' is a true proposition *before* we know that the door is indeed open. We *must* determine the status of the door before we can determine the status of the proposition. Therefore it is not strictly correct to say, 'If the proposition is true, then the door must be open'. Primary knowledge always, always, always, precedes secondary knowledge.

Even if a statement is self-referential, it must contain external (primary) content and not just internal (secondary) content if it is to qualify as a genuine proposition. For example, 'This statement comprises six words' is perfectly acceptable as a proposition because it is making a claim which is external to itself. A sentence, which is a string of words arranged in a particular order, is the vehicle or vessel which conveys or contains the proposition, it is not the proposition itself. As such, it is *external* to the proposition, and is therefore a legitimate subject for a proposition. Should a statement fail to provide any external, or primary, content, then, of logical necessity, it cannot contain any internal, or secondary, content either. If there is no means of generating primary knowledge then there can be no means of generating secondary knowledge. That is to say, truth and falsity are non-existent without the existence of primary knowledge. Truth and falsity are always secondary knowledge; they are an automatic and unvarying response to primary knowledge and are concomitant upon it.

With 'The door is open' we must first test the claim that the proposition makes – *Is* the door open? – and then provide *feedback* on the proposition's own status, true or false. Undoubtedly, primary knowledge is of greater importance as far as knowledge is concerned, so it is 'primary' for two reasons: it is more important and it comes first; and yet secondary knowledge is essential if the proposition is to complete its life-cycle. It is secondary knowledge that transforms the proposition into either a fact or a falsehood at the verification response stage, yet it owes its very existence to the primary knowledge that preceded it.

So, then, what exactly is it that we prove? Do we prove that the door is open (or not), or that the proposition is true (or false), or both of these? What *is* proof and what is the moment of proof? I would argue that the moment of proof is one and the same as the verification moment, and that it is primary knowledge alone that constitutes proof. Of course, if the door is found to be closed, then this constitutes disproof of the proposition's primary content. So really we are considering the moment of proof/disproof.

In order to experience a verification moment, a moment of proof or disproof, we must first have crossed the verification boundary. That is to say, we must have successfully subjected the proposition to an appropriate method of verification, be that an observation, an experiment, a calculation, or whatever, such that it has furnished us with primary knowledge. Naturally, the type of testing that we employ must be recognised as legitimate by our peers and be logically appropriate to the proposition. Should there be a failure in our method of verification and we are unable for whatever reason properly to observe, experiment, calculate, etc., then we will not advance to the verification moment stage and there will be no possibility of proof or disproof. Proof and disproof are nothing other than primary knowledge. Truth and falsity are nothing other than secondary knowledge, which is completely dependent or parasitical upon the primary.

Let me attempt to clarify the point still further, as follows:

	Statement	Observation	V/Moment	V/Response
1.	'The door is open'	The door is open	Proof	True
2.	'The door is open'	The door is closed	Disproof	False

In each of these two cases, the observation leads to a verification moment – a realization – regarding the status of the door. In case 1, the realization that the door is open, when mentally matched to the claim of the statement, constitutes proof and thence elicits the response of 'true' in regard to the statement itself. In case 2, the realization that the door is closed constitutes disproof when mentally matched to the claim of the statement and thence elicits the response of 'false' in regard to the statement itself.

In both instances there has been a *certainty* regarding the status of the door. But too often we term this certainty *proof*. How often do people talk about disproving something or other? Rather, they talk about proving something to be false, or wrong, and this usage of the word 'proof' seems to have a stranglehold on the mental event that I have termed the 'verification moment'. The verification moment is not solely affirmative, it can be affirmative *or* negative.

Going through a reasoning process and reaching an irrefutable conclusion at the end of that process does not necessarily constitute proof. It may, in fact, constitute *dis*proof, the very *opposite* of proof. Proof, therefore, is not to be found in the procedure, nor even in the conclusion. Comparing the conclusion to the claim of the statement (its primary content) is the step that produces proof – or disproof. We therefore need to be very careful indeed regarding the manner in which we use this word 'prove' and its derivatives. We must not use it both to 'prove' that a statement is true and also to 'prove' that a statement is false, which only leads to confusion. The term 'verification moment', as either proof or disproof, can accommodate both these polar opposites, and this is the reason why I choose to use it. Perhaps the word 'determine', though not sufficiently strong or adequate, could be similarly utilized for the reasoning process which reaches an irrefutable conclusion, to incorporate both 'prove' and 'disprove'?

Proposition	Verification Boundary	Verification Moment	Verification Response	Verification Statement
PRIMARY AND SECONDARY CONTENT	become	PRIMARY KNOWLEDGE PROOF or DISPROOF	SECONDARY KNOWLEDGE = TRUE or = FALSE	
Example: 'The door is open' PRIMARY CONTENT = Door is open SECONDARY CONTENT = This statement is factual	becomes or	The door *is* open The door *is* *not* open	True False	

9. Primary and secondary content and knowledge

Doubleness

We are now in a position to address the problem of the 'doubleness' which we encounter in both the Liar and its non-identical twin, 'This statement is true'. Why do we get 'If it is true, it is true; and if it is false, it is false'? The answer has everything to do with primary and secondary content and knowledge.

In the sentence 'This statement is true', there is no genuine primary content. Primary content must refer to the world 'out there', to a state of affairs which is external to the proposition itself. But what do we have in its place? We have secondary knowledge ('true') masquerading as primary content. It is trying to pass itself off as a genuine predicate. Furthermore, it is no longer implicit within the statement, but explicit; no longer a claim, but a supposedly verified fact. So what happens now when we imagine trying to test it? We say, If it is true (primary knowledge), it is true (secondary knowledge); and if it is false (primary knowledge), it is false (secondary knowledge). This is the cause of the 'doubleness'. But we know that both 'true' and 'false' can only ever occur as secondary knowledge, and the point is that secondary knowledge cannot skip its legitimate and necessary place and suddenly become primary knowledge, and worse still, regress even further along the logical chain to become primary content – at least, not if we are dealing with a genuine proposition. For us to determine whether a statement is true or false, as primary knowledge, we would need to know whether it is true or false as secondary knowledge, and yet secondary knowledge is wholly dependent upon primary knowledge for its very existence. There is a loop here, a vicious circularity that can never be resolved, and that is why we will forever say '*If* it is true, or *if* it is false, rather than *it is* true, or *it is* false.

If there is no primary, and secondary is trying to pass itself off as primary, then ultimately, I suppose, what we are left with is not vicious circularity but emptiness. 'This statement is true' is logically incapable of verification, since it is not constructed as a proposition must be. Not only is there malsequence, whereby a 'true' from the post-verification future is cosily settled within it, but during its rough arrival it has also ousted the statement's primary content and is now impersonating it. It is an imposter and it can only cause trouble. The Liar's non-identical twin, then, is destined to remain a neutral statement throughout eternity, and the Liar itself suffers from exactly the same flawed construction. Neither of them have any primary content. Neither of them are propositions.

The Gödel Sentence

At this point I should like to change direction temporarily in order to introduce another element which will prove illuminating in our quest for a thorough understanding of, and solution to, the Liar paradox.

Kurt Gödel (pronounced 'Girdle'), 1906 – 1978, was an Austrian mathematician and logician who fled the Nazis and took American citizenship. Though generally unknown, he is regarded as one of the foremost intellects of the 20th century due to his discovery of the incompleteness theorem, which has had a huge impact in the fields of philosophy, mathematics, computer science, linguistics and many others.

Gödel's Theorem is held to demonstrate that within mathematical systems there are statements which are seemingly true, yet which cannot be proven true within those systems. I wish to utilize a portion of Gödel's discovery as I continue to develop my solution to the Liar paradox. In doing so, I shall find it necessary to modify it slightly, as I need to incorporate it in the true/false trichotomy, which we encountered earlier, and also place it upon a seesaw. I shall explain all as I go along. I hope Gödel doesn't mind too much, but I cannot do this without him. I shall be focusing upon the part of his work which is often called the Gödel sentence.

Here is one – somewhat inaccurate – version of the Gödel sentence that I have seen:

'This statement is true but cannot be proved true.'

Because this statement declares itself to be true, I quite naturally contend that it is inadmissible as a proposition due to malsequence: it is combining a proposition with a verification statement, just as the Liar paradox does. It cannot claim itself to be true in advance of verification.

A more common version of the Gödel sentence, which is a little more faithful to him, runs as follows:

'This statement is not provable.'

No malsequence to be found here – or is there? The usual analysis of this sentence goes something like this: If the statement *is* provable, then it must be a *true* statement, since anything that can be proved must be true. However, if what the statement asserts is true, then it must be exactly as it says it is – not provable. This cannot be, since it would be contradictorily proving itself to be unprovable. If, however, the statement *is not* provable, as it asserts itself to be, and which seems to be the case, then the statement is true. So, what we have here is a statement which is true but unprovable.

However, we must ask, why is it that there is no room for a 'false' anywhere in this analysis? Surely a genuine proposition should be capable of being either true or false? Yet all we seem to have here is a double 'true' under consideration. Further, in working out the above argument to achieve the final 'true', have we not undergone a verification procedure, thereby crossing the verification boundary, experiencing a verification moment and a verification response and then finally issuing the verification statement, 'true'? In other words, have we not in effect *proved* that the statement is unprovable, thus contradicting its claim? And really, isn't this version of the Gödel sentence rather hazy, since what it is actually implying of itself, if not actually making explicit, is 'This statement cannot be proved true.'? (Note this version's similarity to the Strengthened Liar, which we shall briefly consider later on.)

Raymond Smullyan discusses a statement similar to the one above – 'This sentence can never be proved' – and concludes his analysis by remarking, 'Now, I have just proved that the sentence is true. Since the sentence is true, then what it says is really the case, which means that it can never be proved. So how come I have just proved it?'

Professor Smullyan takes this observation no further, yet although he skirts around the issue, he has in fact identified a problem with the 'true' conclusion accorded to this version of the Gödel sentence. There is also an inherent inconsistency in this version so that, in proving itself to be unprovable, it enters the realms of contradiction, of paradox. This is a problem that I shall address shortly. But to my mind there is an additional problem with the above method of verification anyway: it does not follow the correct and logical procedure; and this is the problem that I should like to tackle first.

Following The Correct Verification Procedure

If we test the proposition 'The door is open' and discover that the door *is* open, then the verification response will be 'true'. In *every* case, when the predicate is discovered to be correct in what it asserts, the only response possible is 'true'. Should we discover that the door is closed, the only verification response possible is 'false'. An affirmative always generates a 'true', while a negative always generates a 'false'. These responses are automatic and non-negotiable. If the door *is* open the proposition is true, if the door *is not* open the proposition is false. Always.

If we similarly test 'The door is not open' and determine that the door *is not* open, a 'true' is thereby generated. Should the door be open, a 'false' is the only possible response that can be given. If the door *is not* open the statement is true, if the door *is* open the statement is false. Always.

Because the statement we wish to analyse is about proof, we really do need to clarify how we are going to use this word 'proof' in order to avoid ambiguity and confusion. With 'The door is open', should we say, 'If the door is proved to be open the statement is true, and if the door is proved to be closed the statement is false'? Surely, when we talk about a statement being provable we mean that it can be demonstrated to be exactly as it asserts itself to be?

Proof is affirmative and generates a 'true', disproof is negative and generates a 'false'. Therefore, the correct verification procedure for 'This statement is not provable' should be as follows: If the statement *is not* provable it is true, if it *is* provable it is false. This may appear to be the precise opposite of what we would normally expect, but this most definitely is the correct way of going about it.

So, this being the case, we would now need to *prove* that the statement is not provable in order to generate the 'true' response, but of course this would lead to contradiction, to paradox – the statement would be both provable and not provable simultaneously. Therefore the statement cannot possibly be proved and therefore cannot possibly be true.

However, we must not thereby conclude that, because the statement cannot be proved it is therefore not provable and therefore must be true after all. It is wrong to say, in one breath, that the statement cannot possibly be true and then in the next say that it must be true. If such *is* our response, then we are once again introducing a contradiction at the heart of this statement.

So, let us now bring in the 'false'. Our analysis has demonstrated that 'This statement is not provable' cannot be true. This might suggest to us that therefore it must be false. But for the statement to be false we would need to disprove it; that is to say, we would have to demonstrate that the statement *is* provable. However, were we to achieve this we would encounter yet another contradiction, another paradox, since disproof and proof would once again simultaneously co-exist and a 'true' would be generated to clash with the 'false'.

Two Statements in Parallel

I wish to make this matter as clear as possible, as it can be extremely difficult to keep our thoughts securely on track when considering such statements. Therefore, in order to give ourselves more confidence in the steps that we have just taken, let us look at this Gödel sentence once again, but now in parallel with another, less troublesome, statement. This should help us to see that we are indeed correctly following the verification procedure and not falling into error. As follows:

Statement (a)   **'A square cannot also be a circle.'**
Statement (b)   **'This statement cannot be proved.'**

Step 1
In order for statement (a) to be true, we need to *prove* that a square *cannot* also be a circle.
In order for statement (b) to be true, we need to *prove* that it *cannot* be proved.

Step 2
Statement (a) *can* be proved, both logically and geometrically, and therefore it is true.
Statement (b) can be proved *only* if it cannot be proved, but since this would entail contradiction/paradox, it therefore *cannot* be true.

Step 3

In order for statement (a) to be false, we need to disprove it, that is to say, we need to demonstrate that a square *can* also be a circle.

In order for statement (b) to be false, we need to disprove it, that is to say, we need to demonstrate that it *can* be proved.

Step 4

Statement (a) can be disproved *only* if a square can also be a circle, but since this is logically and geometrically impossible, it therefore *cannot* be false.

Statement (b) can be disproved *only* if it can be proved, but since this would entail contradiction/paradox, it therefore *cannot* be false.

Step 5

Therefore, statement (a) is true.

Therefore, statement (b) is neither true nor false: it is neutral.

Proof, Truth and the Gödel Sentence

Having put our Gödel sentence through a verification procedure and failed to achieve either a true or a false for it, we now stand back from it and, perhaps mentally and informally to ourselves, say, 'That statement *really cannot* be proved!'. Then, correctly, we respond to this *different statement* with a 'true'. We are responding not to the original statement, but to another one, and we must be very, very careful that we do not confuse the two. Unfortunately, I fear that this is indeed what is happening when the Gödel sentence is declared unprovable but true, or true but unprovable.

It is impossible to prove or disprove the statement, 'This statement cannot be proved', and therefore it *cannot* be either true or false. It is neither. It is *neutral*.

I wish to reinforce this conclusion a little more, if I may. Let us recall our experience with the statement, 'The front door of Rose Cottage is open'. Finding that there was no front door at Rose Cottage, we had the *realization* that the statement was not a proposition, since its subject, the door, was missing, and therefore it could not be proved or disproved. This realization was certainly *knowledge* that the door was missing, but it was not *proof* that the door was missing. Proof regarding the missing door could only come in response to the following proposition (or its equivalent), 'The front door of Rose Cottage is missing'. Proof and disproof are responses to a proposition. They are identical to knowledge, but they are knowledge obtained for a specific purpose. Should I for no particular reason walk past Rose Cottage and notice that its front door is missing, I shall have gained knowledge that the door is missing, *but not proof* that the door is missing, since I have not deliberately observed Rose Cottage in response to a proposition regarding it.

Similarly with the Gödel sentence. Having determined that this statement cannot be proved or disproved, we have not *proved* that it cannot be proved or disproved. What *has* occurred is that we have reached a conclusion and have had a *realization*, or gained *knowledge*, that it cannot be proved or disproved, and that therefore it cannot be a proposition. Although proof/disproof and knowledge are more or less identical experiences, they are *technically* different. Thus, when Smullyan asks, 'So how come I have just proved it?', in actuality he has *not* proved it. It is simply that, as a consequence of his reasoning (which is incorrect anyway, because he emerges with a 'true'), he has experienced a realization, a knowledge, that the statement *cannot* be proved and, in error, has mistaken this experience for proof. The very moment we realize the statement cannot be true and cannot be false, is the very moment we should realize it is neutral and cease thinking about it any further, or we will be dragged back into contradictions and erroneous conclusions.

The problem is that the Gödel sentence is suffering from a lack of primary content. Primary content is, as we have suggested, a predicate which is explicit and *external* to the statement itself. Proof is one and the same as affirmative primary knowledge (i.e. we *know* that what the proposition claims to be the case *is* the case), and yet the statement is saying in effect that it cannot cross the verification boundary to yield any such primary knowledge. In other words, it is asserting that, however much we may test it with our powers of reasoning, we will never succeed in proving what it claims of itself.

Gödel did not actually mention the notion of truth in relation to his theorem. *What he did say was that there must be a sentence which is neither provable nor disprovable.*

Therefore, let us take a look at a more authentic version.

'This statement cannot be proved or disproved.'

In effect, this statement is saying that it cannot be declared true or false – it cannot be demonstrated to be either. It is neutral as far as truth-value is concerned, unable as it is to cross the verification boundary. Gödel did not discover a statement that is true but unprovable: for others to declare this to be so is an error. It is an error because it is impossible.

Let us attempt to clarify these matters further. The conclusion 'true', as secondary knowledge, cannot be reached unless primary knowledge has preceded it, i.e. *proof*, since a 'true' or 'false' response to a statement is entirely dependent upon primary knowledge being obtained, as I believe we have already demonstrated. So, to undertake all of these reasoning processes and arrive at the conclusion that the Gödel sentence cannot be proved or disproved and therefore must be true in what it asserts of itself, is to have *proved* that it cannot be proved or disproved, which is in itself a contradiction, a paradox. And not only that: to 'prove' that the sentence cannot be proved or disproved is simultaneously to *disprove* the claims of the sentence, rendering it *false as well as true*. In other words, effectively we are now back to the Liar, back to paradox. Yet now we have a kind of *double* paradox – proof/disproof and true/false! All of this is very confusing and in our attempt to understand it we create nothing but torment for the mind.

I should here like to state a rule that should be reasonably obvious to us: If primary knowledge is obtained then, necessarily, secondary knowledge *must* follow; if secondary knowledge is obtained then, necessarily, primary knowledge *must* have preceded it. Or alternatively expressed: If proof/disproof is obtained then, necessarily, truth/falsity *must* follow; if truth/falsity is obtained then, necessarily, proof/disproof *must* have preceded it. Applying this rule to the Gödel sentence, we can state that it is *impossible* for it to be true without it also having been proven; and if it has been proven then it has simultaneously been disproved and is therefore also false. Paradox.

So our conclusion has to be most definite: should anyone assert any legitimate version of the Gödel sentence to be true, they are *simultaneously* asserting it to be false.

We can say of the Gödel sentence only that it *exists*, and not very much more. It is destined forever to remain on one side of the verification boundary only. Any attempt to wring a 'true' or 'false' from it is futile. It is eternally neutral.

The Gödel sentence cannot achieve a true or false conclusion in regard to itself, just as an eye cannot look upon itself. It is a verification blind spot. But just as a mirror will enable an eye to see itself as it is, so we can use another statement to enable us to comment upon the Gödel sentence, as we have earlier intimated. Thus, if we state, for example, 'There is a statement which cannot be proved or disproved', we can respond to this with an accurate 'True'. However, it is important to acknowledge that this 'true' can only be achieved with external assistance and that it applies to a different statement, not to the Gödel sentence itself. We can only do this by moving outside and looking back in, so to speak.

It is also important to realize that the neutrality which we are ascribing to the Gödel sentence does not violate the law of excluded middle, provided we accept that this law applies solely to all propositions and not to all statements, which I believe we must. We need to remember that propositions are just one of three types of statement, as demonstrated in the structure of the true/false trichotomy. *All* statements are neutral anyway, unless and until they cross the verification boundary. If a statement cannot cross this boundary – i.e. it cannot be successfully tested – then it remains forever neutral. The Gödel sentence is one such example. It has not been successfully tested and *as a consequence* found to be neutral; rather, it is not amenable to testing, as a proposition is, and that is *why* it is neutral. It is not amenable to testing because proving it will also have the consequence of disproving it, and vice versa. (Recall the athlete, Gödel Sentence, who try as she might can never cross the finishing line because it is forever moving away from her?) Gödel's paper of 1931, *On Formally Undecidable Propositions of Principia Mathematica and Related Systems* should, at least from our perspective, be renamed *On Formally Neutral Statements* ...

Other statements of the Gödel kind could be, 'This statement cannot cross the verification boundary'; 'This statement has neutral truth-value'. There are possibly quite a few others, and all are asserting basically the same thing regarding themselves. The Gödel sentence, then, is not an 'undecidable proposition' as Gödel himself declares it to be; rather, it is an eternally neutral statement and not a proposition at all.

Another Form of the Gödel Sentence

Adapting the Gödel sentence slightly, for the purposes of my argument, I shall recast it as the following, yet without in any way modifying its essence:

Proposition	Verification Boundary	Verification Moment	Verification Response	Verification Statement
THE GÖDEL SENTENCE				
This statement cannot be proved or disproved	**Logical reasoning**	Proof unobtainable	Therefore cannot be true	
Not a Proposition	Statement cannot cross this boundary	Disproof unobtainable	Therefore cannot be false	
No primary content		Therefore no primary knowledge	Therefore no secondary knowledge	
Eternally Neutral				

10. Analysis of the Gödel sentence

'This statement is neither true nor false.'

The reasons why there is no difference between the above statement and the Gödel sentence are as follows:

'This statement cannot be proved or disproved.'

equals

'This statement cannot yield any primary knowledge.'

and

'This statement is neither true nor false.'

equals

'This statement cannot yield any secondary knowledge.'

These two are equivalent, since, as we have already discovered, primary knowledge (proof/disproof) *must* generate secondary knowledge (true/false), and secondary knowledge *must* have been preceded by primary knowledge. Primary and secondary knowledge are inextricably linked: if you have either one, you *must* have the other; if you lack either one, you *must* lack the other.

What, then, can we say about 'This statement is neither true nor false'? It exists. It exists as a statement, is *neutral*, and has no truth-value whatever. We must resist the very real temptation to rush over and declare it true. It is not true. It exists and is valid as a statement, is all we can say. It is certainly not a proposition, since it is not 'capable of being true or false'. We can look at it. We can understand it. But we cannot categorise it in any way, shape or form as being true. It is as intriguing in its own way as the Liar paradox. As long as we appreciate that it is only the type of statement known as a proposition that needs to be either true or false and not every type of statement, we shall begin to grow more comfortable with this state of affairs.

With all of this in mind, let us now move on to test statement (b) from the true/false trichotomy, which should result in precisely the same conclusions as for the Gödel sentence we have just examined, for the simple reason that they are virtually identical.

'This statement is neither true nor false.'

This statement cannot be neutral if it yields a 'true'. It cannot be neutral if it yields a 'false'. To be neutral the statement must be logically incapable of crossing the verification boundary at all. If it cannot cross the boundary this will irrefutably demonstrate that the statement is not a proposition and hence must be neutral as far as truth-value is concerned. Here we go, then.

'This statement is neither true nor false.'

If we first of all change this to the equivalent, 'This statement is neutral', i.e. has no truth-value, this will avoid lots of 'true's and 'false's floating around and confusing us. So:

'This statement is neutral.'

If the statement can be proved to be neutral (primary knowledge), then it is true (secondary knowledge), but if true it is not neutral. It cannot be both true and neutral. To disprove the statement, i.e. to demonstrate that it is not neutral, would mean that the statement can be shown to be either true or false, as *primary knowledge*, before responding to the statement with a 'false', as secondary knowledge. In other words, if the statement is either true or false then it is false. Well now, we have seen that true/false cannot be primary knowledge, and so this attempt to achieve such a result cannot ever succeed. If we shift this over to the right (as far as figure 9. is concerned), from primary to secondary where truth and falsity really belong, we find that now we have a totally empty slot for primary knowledge, and with nothing at all to fill it, and so the whole process collapses. We must therefore conclude that the statement can never be proved to be true or disproved to be false and is therefore genuinely neutral. The statement 'This statement is neither true nor false' is not true, it just *is*. Again, we must be careful to resist the notion that we have just *proved* this statement to be neutral, for that would entail the statement being true, *and* also false.

Time now to see where and why the Gödel sentence is included in the true/false trichotomy, how it sits in relation to propositions and paradoxes, and whereabouts it will be placed on the soon-to-be-seen seesaw, which, of course, also needs to have its arrival explained.

The True/False Trichotomy Again

'True' and 'false' are polar opposites, with no shades in between. Propositions cannot be partially true or partially false, else they need to be restructured in order to yield the *whole* truth-value. Either/or. This or that. One or the other. Now, if we work out the various permutations that both 'true' and 'false' can be involved in, we discover that there are only three. These three, which I have labelled (a), (b) and (c) for the sake of convenience, are, as we saw earlier, as follows:

STATEMENT	TYPE	STATUS
(a) Either true or false	PROPOSITION	CONSISTENT
(b) Neither true nor false	GÖDEL SENTENCE	NEUTRAL
(c) Both true and false	LIAR PARADOX	INCONSISTENT

11. The true/false trichotomy again

As can be seen, each of the above components of the trichotomy acts as a blueprint or prototype for one of the three types of statement with which we are currently concerned.

Component (a) matches perfectly the options open or available to a *proposition*, and therefore we declare it to be descriptive of this statement type. It honours the law of non-contradiction and an excluded middle is nowhere to be seen. This is exactly as we would expect it to be, because these laws of logic are actually the laws that govern the statement type known as a proposition.

If all statements were propositions, then we would feel compelled to reject most firmly component (b), since all propositions must be either true or false. Yet we cannot so respond. Such a reaction would merely be an expression of our own preconceptions or prejudices and would not be based on the reality of the facts before us. Whereas (a) has an inner potential, we might say, for becoming or looking towards something else – producing a true or false –, (b) can never be anything other than it already is: neutral. The Gödel sentence will take a central (literally!) role when we come to look at the seesaw. This statement type *does not* honour the law of excluded middle, though it does not need to, since it is not a proposition, yet it *does* bow before the law of non-contradiction, since there is nothing contradictory in it. However, because of its neutrality, this sentence *is* the excluded middle that is so feared in relation to propositions. 'This statement is neither true nor false' is the Gödel sentence in one of its purest forms: imperturbable and in perfect equilibrium. What Gödel unwittingly discovered was not an undecidable proposition but the second type of statement in the true/false trichotomy.

Component (c) violates just about everything around. This statement type is on a drunken night out. It asserts of itself that it is true, and so has fallen into malsequence; but doubly so, for this further implies that it is also false. This cannot be a proposition. This cannot be the Gödel sentence. This must be the Liar paradox which, as we have already seen, is a hybrid sentence formed from a proposition and a verification statement. The law of non-contradiction is being laughed at; having beer thrown in its face!

The Gödel Sentence and the Verification Boundary

Because of its neutrality, the Gödel sentence to some degree *is* the verification boundary. The verification boundary in some sense *is* the Gödel sentence. They are almost one and the same. As neutral zero marks the boundary between positive and negative numbers, as the neutral zone in a bar magnet marks the boundary between the North and South poles, so, too, does the neutral Gödel sentence mark the boundary between true and false. There *must* be an area of neutrality. There *must* be a neutral Gödel sentence. However, the verification boundary can be distinguished slightly from the Gödel sentence in the sense that it marks the outer limit of the sentence, where the neutrality of a proposition meets the point of its verification – the verification moment.

Gödel is the neutral zone occupied by all propositions, but its far-most limit is the point at which a verification procedure – a test, experiment, observation, calculation, etc. – is performed *and a result obtained*. The verification moment, the point when it is realized that 'The door is open' or 'The door is not open', signals the end of the boundary, that it has been crossed, that the neutral zone of Gödel has been left behind and that now a 'true' or 'false' is about to be achieved.

The person undergoing this experience, the *knower*, will now mentally transfer the proposition 'The door is open' to the other side of the verification boundary, where it will become a fact or a falsehood. For a person who has not yet tested the proposition, whom we might designate the *wonderer*, it will remain on the neutral side of the verification boundary, as a proposition. Thus we have the self-same statement being perceived in two entirely different ways. Relativity.

If the wonderer subsequently tests the proposition for him or herself, he or she, too, will experience the very same 'events' and the proposition will undergo an identical metamorphosis and become a fact or a falsehood, both of which inhabit post-verification territory. Of course, all of this is occurring in the human consciousness and there are no labels or signposts or marked boundaries or lines of demarcation anywhere to be seen; yet the various states and conditions I have depicted and named do, I believe, accurately reflect what really does take place within the human consciousness when a proposition is considered, put to the test, and then responded to.

The Gödel sentence/verification boundary, expressed as 'This statement is neither true nor false', is, as I have said, a neutral zone. It encompasses within itself all propositions, which in themselves are neither true nor false. However, propositions can be progressed further if so desired. Yes, they can remain in the neutral zone throughout all eternity if no one bothers to subject them to the rigours of a verification procedure. But if testing is to take place they can move within the neutral zone to push up hard against the verification boundary. At this point, if the claim the proposition makes is demonstrated to be true or false its life will be over and it will become, for the knower at least, something else (i.e. a fact or a falsehood) – the caterpillar will have become a butterfly.

But if, at the point of verification, we discover that the so-called proposition is not a real proposition at all, then there will be no butterfly fluttering within our consciousness today, nor even a caterpillar crawling by. Earlier we considered the proposition, 'The front door of Rose Cottage is open', and argued that, if Rose Cottage did not have a front door, we could not declare the statement to be either true or false. In such circumstances, it was said, the so-called proposition would have to be demoted to the rank of statement, being either an inadmissible statement, a failed proposition or a pseudo-proposition – take your pick of the names. Whatever we may prefer to call such a statement, we can now see that it has moved within its abstract neutral zone, to push against the verification boundary, but has failed to cross it, and has been repulsed. Had it been a well-constructed proposition it would have included a location in time as well as in space, rendering it very specific. But this statement is now doomed to eternal rest in the neutral zone, never to escape, in exactly the same manner as the Gödel sentence. For to modify its location in time in order to take account of Rose Cottage's door subsequently being returned, would be to create an entirely new (or genuine) proposition, which could then successfully challenge the verification boundary.

Have I forgotten all about the Liar paradox? Not at all. I shall soon be discussing how there are other factors involved in the generation of this paradox and not solely malsequence.

But first! I need to borrow something from the world of physics, and from the branch known as mechanics in particular.

The Seesaw

I would like to introduce a seesaw into our examination of the Liar. Not because I believe that the human consciousness harbours some kind of abstract seesaw or anything resembling it, but because I do believe that truth, falsity and neutrality operate according to many of the same principles which govern the functioning of a seesaw. I think there are benefits to be had by employing something that is very familiar to us in order to illuminate something else that is not. What follows is not going to be a difficult physics lesson, but a very simple depiction of what goes on in the seesaw world.

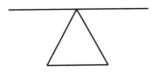

12. The seesaw world

Here is a plank of wood supported in its very centre by a pin or shaft which allows either side of the plank to move up or down. If everything has been constructed to perfection – that is, with very great precision – the plank, at rest, will be parallel to the ground on both sides. Let us regard this state of equilibrium as the *neutral* position. Only two other positions are possible in our seesaw world, as illustrated below.

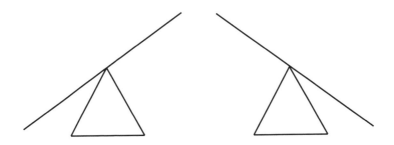

13. Two more possibilities in the seesaw world

Yes, there are many levels of up and down in between equilibrium and the plank's contact with the ground on one side or the other, but I wish to consider only these two states, since the limit of the seesaw's movement has been reached when it makes contact with the ground. Contact point is what interests me for the purpose of this analogy.

It is stating the obvious, but note how, when one side leaves the condition of equilibrium and makes contact with the ground, the other side also leaves equilibrium and is in a condition *opposite* to that of contact. Quite simple, really: when the left-hand side is down the right-hand side is up, and vice versa, or there is a state of equilibrium whereby both sides cancel each other out and the plank runs parallel to the ground. The fulcrum, or pivot, is, we might say, the mediator in all of this; it is the source of all action or inaction; it 'holds the balance of power'. The fulcrum sits betwixt the polar opposites: hence the term, 'pivotal'.

Now let us apply 'true' and 'false' to the seesaw, also the Gödel sentence, and let them be accompanied by positive/negative numbers and zero: they all belong to the same logical family.

Proposition

Zero

Neutral

Verification

Gödel Boundary Sentence

True   False
+1   -1

14. The seesaw in neutral mode

The above diagram illustrates the position a seesaw would occupy if it were to represent a proposition, which is neutral – neither true nor false at this moment, but which has the capability of being either true or false. Indeed, the seesaw *must* tip one way or another when the proposition is tested. Note that the Gödel sentence, or neutrality, is the perfect state of equilibrium, the whole of the plank, while the verification boundary is located at the fulcrum – *is* the fulcrum. Also featured are the elements of the law of trichotomy from the mathematical world: +1,-1 and zero, which precisely mirror true, false and neutral; they are all natural cousins.

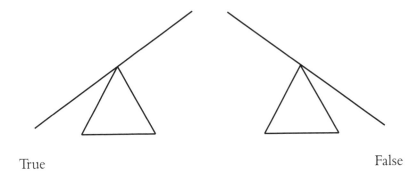

True   False

15. The seesaw with true and false propositions

When a verification procedure is completed, a realization of the proposition's truth-value is obtained, equilibrium/neutrality is lost and the proposition is declared true or false. It can be seen from the above illustrations that neutrality has disappeared in both cases and a 'true' or a 'false' value has appeared. When the left-hand side of the seesaw makes contact with the ground to be declared 'true', the opposite side also leaves the neutral zone but travels in the opposite direction and is rendered inactive, out of contention. Unlike on an ordinary physical seesaw, however, which can alternately move up and down, these positions, once determined, remain permanent. True for all time or false for all time.

If we now place the three trichotomy statements on the seesaw, each in their turn, we shall observe the following.

(a) Either true or false

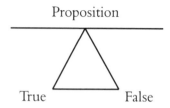

(b) Neither true nor false

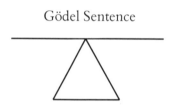

(c) Both true and false

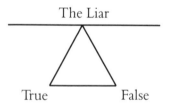

16. The true/false trichotomy on the seesaw

Component (a) is the blueprint for a proposition. A statement of this type is currently neutral and therefore in perfect equilibrium, yet is poised to tip either to one side or the other as true or false once it has been successfully tested.

Component (b) is the blueprint for a Gödel sentence. It is currently and eternally neutral, therefore in perfect equilibrium, and ever will remain so. True and false are not indicated as they are unachievable.

Component (c), as we have previously noted, seems to contravene just about every rule around. So why, if it is supposed to be both true and false, is the statement in a condition of neutrality, of equilibrium? Why is the seesaw not thrashing wildly up and down, up and down, up and down, like a Belisha beacon flashing on and off, on and off, on and off? If it is true, it is false; and if it is false, it is true, and so on, and so on.

This is what I shall endeavour to explain now. It may be something of a relief to know that I am drawing closer to tying up all the loose ends and to declaring the Liar paradox solved. I shall have to hope that the explanations I offer, which satisfy all of *my* questions, will also satisfy *yours*.

Tralse

Let us return to our original problem, the Liar paradox, and 'This statement is false'. Vicious circularity is supposed to kick in because we go round and round in a giddy-spin, saying, 'If it is true, it is false; and if it is false, it is true, and if it is true, it is false; and if ...' and so on, forever, if we are crazy enough to allow it. I have likened the effect more to a Belisha beacon, which flashes on and off repeatedly. The truth, however, is that neither of these responses turns out to be at all accurate when we thoroughly get to the bottom of what is really going on. We go endlessly round and round in a vicious circle, or flash interminably on and off, because psychologically those are the only ways in which our minds can cope with the implications of the Liar paradox, but in the terms of the paradox itself these effects should not happen at all.

17. Belisha beacon on; Belisha beacon off

Why? Because 'If it is true, it is false; and if it is false, it is true' etc. are true and false *alternately*, whereas in reality the true and false are *concurrent, simultaneous*. What we have here is not first one and then the other, but *both at the same time*. The Liar paradox demands that both true and false are active *together*. The instant that we have 'true' is the instant that we have 'false'. What we should really experience, then, is a fusion of the two, true and false, which we could more accurately record, and refer to, as *tralse*. The Liar paradox generates tralse, not true and false (which separately are all our minds are capable of handling), and tralse is a permanent state of the two with no oscillations, no variations. *This* is why the seesaw remains in the neutral position. If true and false have equal 'weight' as polar opposites, then when they are placed on the two sides of the seesaw at precisely the same instant, they would effect no movement of it. There would be a condition of stasis, immobility – no movement at all.

Of course, in the physical world a normal seesaw would break in half if the two weights placed upon it were heavy enough; but this being the case the apparatus remaining would no longer be a seesaw – thus:

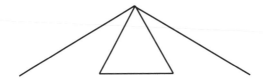

18. The broken seesaw

This is what 'This statement is both true and false' is trying to achieve, with the two sides, left and right, contacting the ground as true and false. But our mental seesaw is made of sturdier stuff and *cannot* be broken. This is the reason why we witness the state of equilibrium. Though the pressure may be great, neutrality holds, and two great laws of logic are left inviolate, triumphant.

However, this is not how some modern logicians see it. Dialetheists argue that we should cease trying to remove every inconsistency and contradiction from propositions and accept that sometimes we simply have to live with them. For the dialetheists, the Liar is a tolerable oddity; annoying, perhaps, but really no big deal. They would accept that, occasionally, there can be a proposition which is both true and false, and perhaps would look benignly upon our broken seesaw. We have to ask whether theirs is a genuine position (though without much logical foundation in support of it), or whether, having found the Liar paradox intractable, they have simply given up.

If we were to accept that true and false can co-exist we would also have to accept that the front door of Rose Cottage can be both open and closed at the very same instant (not alternately open and closed); that a light can be simultaneously on *and* off (not alternately on and off). For we have always to bear in mind that what we call true and false are nothing substantial in themselves; they are *mental responses only* and have no independent existence of their own. After all, the verification moment is really but an experience of *knowing* something, not verifying something.

For example, if there had been no proposition, spoken or written, about the front door of Rose Cottage being open, then, when I turn the corner and see that the front door of the cottage is open or closed, I do not have a verification moment at all, because I am not seeking to affirm or deny something that has been written or spoken. At this point, truth and falsity do not even enter my mind and there will be no verification response. What I *do* have is the knowledge that the door is open or closed because I have just now observed this to be the case, yet it is unlikely that I will pause to think that this knowledge is in any way significant. We have thousands of such moments every day. Significance arises only when propositions (or questions) are involved, and I have labelled this experience the verification moment simply because we are here dealing with propositions. We could just as easily call this experience the 'moment of knowing' or anything else that is descriptive and meaningful. Truth and falsity do not exist where propositions do not exist. They are a 'correct' or an 'incorrect', an 'affirmative' or a 'negative', a tick or a cross. That is all they are. They feed off propositions. But two mouths cannot suck at the same teat at the same time. Either/or. One or the other. This or that. The dialetheists are wrong.

We are incapable of conceiving the nature of tralse, and this is why mentally we alternate between the states of true and false. There is no such thing as a square circle, though we can speak of it as if there were. Yet, not only does a square circle not exist in the physical world, it cannot even be created conceptually. Unlike a yellow circle or a circle with a 5 centimetre diameter, we simply cannot imagine it. All we *can* do is, for example, imagine a square within a circle, or a circle within a square, or imagine them interlocked or standing side by side or with one above the other, and so on. A square and a circle simply will not fuse; they are logically and geometrically mutually exclusive. Probably the closest that we can get to fusion is the 'squircle', which is sometimes characterised as a square with rounded corners, but this product of the two is neither a square nor a circle and falls far short of what is intended.

The condition I have called 'tralse' is equivalent to a square circle: it does not exist. As with a square circle, we can talk about it, but this is a case of language failing to match reality. Our unwitting acceptance of malsequence and willingness to let it lead us where it will, inevitably brings us to tralse, though we fail to recognize it for what it is. On/off, this/that, is all our minds are capable of – and rightly so, with the seesaw up or down, otherwise it will be broken, together with our mental health. Thus are we further seduced into believing that a true or false value can be obtained for the Liar paradox. But when we finally realize that tralse actually entails neutrality, the paradox disappears. We witness the death of this paradox and are relieved to discover that logic, reason and common sense remain secure.

The Big 'If'

We say '*If* it is true, it is false; and *if* it is false, it is true …' We do not say 'It *is* true, so it *is* false; and it *is* false, so it *is* true …' And why do we do this? We do this because the Liar is beyond any kind of verification procedure; it cannot cross the verification boundary because it would thereby only achieve an eternal state of equilibrium. True and false, because they are concurrent, not alternate, would cancel each other out if the verification boundary were to be traversed. But crossing the verification boundary absolutely *must* result in a realization of either true or false – that is how the proposition system works, just like a seesaw – and for the Liar paradox this is an impossibility, since it is not a proposition, as we have already demonstrated.

The dreaded excluded middle, which everyone is anxious to avoid at all costs, cannot be ignored. But it is not to be feared. It is the state of neutrality occupied by all propositions at all times. It is the ground occupied by the Liar paradox. It is the permanent home of the Gödel sentence. It is a *pre*-verification place, not a *post*-verification place. It *precedes* the manifestation of true or false, it does not situate itself *between* true and false. For this reason, our analogy of a two-dimensional seesaw cannot accurately represent the real state of affairs. The analogy of the car racing ahead and then turning either left or right when it crosses the white line is probably more accurate, since it portrays the state of neutrality more clearly as being in a different *dimension* to that of true and false, and antecedent to it. As a result of our analysis, the excluded middle has been given a makeover and a new name.

At this point I would assert that, in reality, there is no paradox. The Liar sentence never achieves genuine contradiction. It is an 'if' but never an 'is'. 'This statement is false' draws to the very brink of contradiction, of paradox, yet it does not cross over and become one. It cannot. We human beings create the paradox by first of all introducing malsequence into a sentence, creating a hybrid, which both logically and naturally is disallowed; then we spread the infection by speculating with an 'if'; and finally we compound our developing madness by failing to realize that the seesaw of truth and falsity can be either one or the other, but not both. In treating the Liar as a regular proposition we are forcing it to yield a true or a false, when it is incapable of such, since it is not a proposition. It is of another statement type, as we have seen by contemplating the true/false trichotomy. Thus is the law of non-contradiction vindicated as sound and unassailable. Thus is the law of excluded middle able to sigh with relief.

With the Liar, malsequence has poisoned our minds and led us into dark labyrinths of insanity where human beings are not supposed to set foot.

The Strengthened Liar

The Strengthened Liar is supposed to be an even tougher version of the Liar paradox and is reputed to confound any approach which has achieved at least some success in addressing the Liar. If the analysis that I have developed in these pages rests upon secure foundations, then even this Strengthened Liar should submit to it and be vanquished. Let us see what happens, then. Here it is.

'This statement is not true.'

Straightaway, we can identify the presence of malsequence, because a 'true' outcome is denied in advance of verification. A genuine proposition must be capable of being true or false. This statement is not a genuine proposition but a hybrid, part proposition, part verification statement. For reasons already explained, such a combination is forbidden, so we would be perfectly within our rights to walk away from it: it is a pip with an apple growing out from it, with no tree anywhere in sight!

However, if it really is such a tough character, let us tackle it and see if it is tough enough to demolish our two very important laws of logic. Here we go, then.

First of all, I wish to take issue with the accepted response to this statement, which runs something like this.

'This statement is not true.'

If this statement is true, then it is exactly as it asserts itself to be, namely, not true. On the other hand, if the statement is not true, then it is precisely what it claims itself to be, and hence it is true.

Here again we have lost a 'false' somewhere along the line, just as we did with a version of the Gödel sentence. The statement is making a claim regarding itself and, if we are going to treat it exactly the same as any other regular proposition (and let us not forget that these paradoxes are indeed considered bona fide propositions), we must be looking for values of either true or false only, nothing else, since nothing other than these two is permitted. After all, 'not true' may imply 'false', yet it could also indicate neutrality, which is impermissible for a proposition. So, we need to correct this infelicity.

With this in mind, let us turn again to the Strengthened Liar, follow the correct verification procedure, and see what the real outcomes should be.

'This statement is not true.'

If this statement *is* not true (i.e. it is false, but not neutral as this is impermissible) then it is true, and if this statement *is not* not true (i.e. it *is* true) then it is false. We have descended into absurdity once again and experience the true/false fusion of tralse, exactly the same as with the Liar.

Does the Strengthened Liar present any terrors for us or produce any insurmountable difficulties? The answer must be No – it reduces to the Liar, for which we have already provided our solution, so why it is termed *strengthened* is something of a mystery. Nor does the Truth-teller ('This statement is true.') back us into any corners; neither the fourth and final alternative, 'This statement is not false'. Analyzing these latter two (far weaker) statements would be pointless. We know that all four are defective, fundamentally flawed hybrids that automatically disqualify themselves from undergoing a verification procedure, since they are not propositions.

A similar paradox to the Liar employs two sentences in order to achieve the same effect. On one side of a piece of paper is written the statement, 'The sentence on the other side of this sheet of paper is false', and on the reverse is written, 'The sentence on the other side of this sheet of paper is true'. But the self-referential nature of the twin statements means that they can be reduced to just one sentence, i.e. 'This statement is both true and false'. Well, we now know how to respond to this!

Back to the Olympics

It may be appropriate at this point to revisit our Olympic friends. It should be clear to us by now that Proposition has no greater status than Question, for they both occupy the neutral zone and the race has yet to be run.

Liar Paradox, we can now with certainty state, is totally delusional, since she is attempting to insert the race result of tomorrow into the middle of today – and this absolutely cannot be done. We were foolish ever to entertain her declarations; but now we can more easily resist her intellectual charms.

Verification Statement may well very much resemble Proposition at times, especially when, for example, she responds to 'The door is open' by stating that 'The door *is* open'. Yet she has never run a race in her life and never will; she works on the other side of the finishing line and usually reports back to us with a 'true' or a 'false', a 'correct' or an 'incorrect', or with words that have the same value. But not once can we place our trust in Verification Statement or grant her our total confidence.

Gödel Sentence is a sorry athlete, since she cannot really even begin the race, let alone hope to win it or even complete it. She should perhaps remove her athlete's vest and resolve to settle for a much quieter life.

Perhaps I could offer a few final words about propositions before we move on to a different type of paradox. Propositions can only point the way to knowledge, they cannot contain or convey knowledge. This is because knowing is a private mental event which is non-transferable. If I say I know that water boils at 100° Celsius at sea level, what I really mean is that I have placed my trust in the integrity of those scientists who have performed this experiment and I *very strongly believe* in their results or am *convinced* by their results; that I am highly confident I could perform the same experiment and achieve an identical outcome: I have knowledge by proxy. But until I *do* perform such an experiment I cannot truly *know* that water boils at a particular temperature at sea level. For absolute certainty I *must* cross the verification boundary for myself. There is no alternative. Genuine knowledge cannot be wrapped up in little language parcels and passed from one person to another.

THE BARBER OF
SEVILLE

You are peering through the large window of a barber shop in the village of Seville. It is shortly before 9.00 am and the barber will soon be opening up for business. You are full of excitement and anticipation because you have just spotted the barber inside the shop and have noted that he still has stubble on his chin. The barber is always clean-shaven when he welcomes his first customer of the day, so you are convinced that any minute now you will witness a momentous event and finally solve the riddle that has bamboozled every other investigator thus far. For it is said that the barber works in accordance with a very strict rule, as follows:

'The Barber of Seville shaves all and only those men of Seville who do not shave themselves.'

So the big question that everyone has been asking is, Does the Barber of Seville shave himself? If he does, he doesn't; and if he doesn't, he does. With just a few minutes remaining before the shop is due to open, the barber is bound to have his stubble removed any second now – but who is going to do it? You watch intently …

At this very moment a good friend rushes up to you, breathless, and urges you to abandon your quest because there is something far more exciting about to take place in the next village down the road and she has only just heard about it. Apparently, for an hour each day, and starting at 9.00 am, Jake the Executioner beheads all and only those people in his village who do not behead themselves. Hardly surprisingly, after a great deal of bloodshed, word has got round and all the remaining villagers have fled. Since Jake is now the only person left in the village he must now wield the axe against himself. Or must he? If he does behead himself, he doesn't; and if he doesn't, he does. The outcome of this puzzle is sure to be far more interesting than that of a nondescript little barber, your friend suggests, and she urges you to join her. You ponder. Bothered at the prospect of copious blood and gore, you politely decline – and off your friend shoots! You resume your watch, certain that the slicing off of bristles will be far more pleasant to witness than the slicing off of heads. You see the barber pick up a razor. His assistant also has one. And then …

The Barber of Seville paradox was devised by the English philosopher Bertrand Russell in 1918 and is linked to a problem he had discovered in set theory, which we will examine in due course. R. M. Sainsbury responds to this paradox by dismissing it as 'not very deep' and by declaring that such a barber cannot exist, yet without in any way getting to grips with the paradox. I should like to challenge this interpretation. I do not accept that it is a paradox of little consequence and believe that upon further investigation it will yield some very profitable logical insights.

Back to the Trichotomy

There are obvious similarities between the Liar and the Barber. Both are concerned with polar opposites – the Liar with true/false, the Barber with shaves himself/does not shave himself. We can therefore call upon the true/false trichotomy to aid us in our treatment of the Barber paradox. We can employ it because this trichotomy cannot claim to be exclusive to the true/false problem: it may be applied to any pair of polar opposites where an either/or situation obtains. Perhaps in its more general application we could rename it the trichotomy of opposites (which I think sounds rather nice) and its three components could run something like this:

(Where a and b are polar opposites)

(1) Either a or b	CONSISTENT
(2) Neither a nor b	NEUTRAL
(3) Both a and b	INCONSISTENT

19. The trichotomy of opposites

So, then, let us get down to business by first of all matching our barber against the trichotomy, and then try to determine exactly what is going on.

Let us deal with the neutral part (2), 'Neither a nor b', first. The barber could be unaffected by the problem of whether or not he shaves himself in at least four circumstances, in which case there will be no paradox:

1. He cannot grow facial hair and therefore has no need to shave
2. He wears a beard which he never shaves
3. He is not a man of Seville – he only works in Seville, he does not live there
4. The barber is not a man but a woman

We can readily see that, if the paradox is to bite, we need to exclude any possibility of an opt-out and do away with neutrality. There is therefore a need to tighten the paradox since in its present form it is inadequate. The barber *must* be made to shave.

A revised rule might look something like this: 'The Barber of Seville (who is a man, a resident of Seville, and shaves regularly) shaves all those beardless men of Seville who do not shave themselves'. It may look clumsy and contrived, but it serves the purpose – and anyway, most paradoxes *are* contrived.

Part (1), 'Either a or b', next. The men of Seville who do not shave themselves may well be shaved by a wife, another relative, a friend, a colleague, etc. In order for the paradox to work there cannot be one of these third alternatives: a man of Seville must either shave himself or be shaved by the Barber of Seville – not just because the rule says so, but to ensure it is being done as a matter of demonstrable fact. Either/or. One or the other. This or that. But first the barber would need to determine which men of Seville shave themselves. Let us suppose that all clean-shaven men (aged eighteen or over?) gather outside the barber's shop one morning and those of them who do regularly shave themselves now proceed to demonstrate this fact to the barber. These men may now be crossed off the barber's list of men who must be shaved by him.

But how can you ensure that all the remaining men *are* shaved by the barber? This can only be achieved by consent or compulsion – and then the barber must shave *all* of them. He must shave all of them because the paradox rule specifically asserts that the Barber of Seville shaves all of these men. 'Shaves', in the present tense, implies this is already being done, not that it is hoped or intended that it will be done. If the paradox rule were to assert that the Barber of Seville 'will shave' these men, there can be no prospect of paradox for the time being. Intention does not equate to accomplishment.

So, then, let us suppose that the barber has indeed achieved the great feat of shaving all those clean-shaven men of Seville who do not shave themselves. We now come to the third component of our trichotomy: 'Both a and b'.

EITHER / OR   NEITHER / NOR

The Barber sentence has been further and further
tightened in order to squeeze it
towards inescapable
paradox
BOTH

The word *only* in the paradox rule, together with the *all*, are obviously the factors which now push and shove the poor barber towards paradox. He is a man of Seville. He is clean-shaven. He is included in the 'all'. So he performs the seemingly impossible and both shaves himself and does not shave himself – *simultaneously*! As we have already seen with the Liar, alternation between the polar opposites does not make for paradox. Paradox does not want this or that, one or the other; it demands this *and* that, one *and* the other, and both *at the same time*.

And so to our third component, 'Both a and b'. The barber is here being compelled into a position of paradox, whereby he shaves himself and yet does not shave himself. This is equivalent to tralse, and earlier in this book I argued that tralse did not result in the conflict of paradox, but in the paralysis of neutrality, a mid-point or pivot, where neither of the polar opposites was active. If we apply the Barber paradox to the seesaw we can see that neutrality is indeed the case here also.

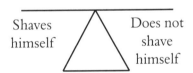

20. The Barber of Seville on the seesaw.

However, having stripped the barber of his neutrality, since he definitely does shave, we cannot possibly consider the paradox to be anywhere near being solved. If the barber is definitely shaving, then who is doing it – he himself, or someone else? And in so doing, are the terms of the rule being obeyed or violated?

The Big If – Again!

Here we are again, exactly as it was with the Liar: If it is true, it is false; if it is false, it is true; if he does shave himself, he doesn't; if he doesn't, he does. We do not have: The barber *is* shaving himself and therefore *not* shaving himself; and because he *is not* shaving himself he *is* shaving himself. All we have is a kind of dreamy speculation which bears no relation to the real world. The delight is in the conflict the statement generates and there is no proper consideration of the way in which reality is apparently being twisted to suit the needs of the rule rather than the reverse, in which the rule is made to serve reality.

If the barber *is* shaving, whether by his own hand or that of another, he is *already* breaking the terms of the rule. Though this is not quite accurate. In order to break a rule it must be possible for such a rule to be implemented and adhered to in the first place. The rule expressed by the Barber paradox seemingly cannot *ever* be implemented or adhered to, so there is no rule for the barber to break. The rule simply cannot become current or operational. This paradox is yet another square circle: easy to talk about, but absolutely incapable of being conceptualised in the mental world or manifested in the material world. It is the *rule* that does not exist, not the barber. Reality forbids 'Both a and b' and language needs to reflect this fact and bow down before it. Reality is king, not language.

Once again the great law of non-contradiction has been challenged and once again it has seen off its aggressor. The servant persists in trying to become the master, yet is always vanquished.

Self-Reference and the Fulcrum

The Barber of Seville is in the thick of things. He is the one doing the shaving or not doing the shaving. Because of his unique position he qualifies for an exemption from any rule which pertains to those people either side of him – those whom he shaves and those whom he does not shave. It needs to be well understood that the barber is the fulcrum on the seesaw with the polar opposites, the shaved and the not shaved, to his left and to his right. He really *must* remain neutral, poised between the two. He cannot be both sides of the seesaw as well as its pivot. Therefore, any rule that is drawn up is duty-bound and reality-bound to take account of his unique position and exclude him from its influence. He occupies an identical position to that of the Gödel sentence: neutral.

But let us tarry awhile. Let us not be so quick to depart from this paradox and assume it to be solved, when really it is still something of a blur. Let us try another line of attack.

We have squeezed the barber nearer and nearer to paradox by apparently denying him all escape routes. As part of this process, we have also ensured – insisted – that he is not treated as a special case, that he conforms to the expectations placed upon all other men of Seville; and indeed, we have been forced to impose severe restrictions upon the shaving options available to the men of Seville. But the fact is that – as already stated – the barber is not and cannot be, an equal partner in this arrangement, for the reasons depicted immediately below.

GROUP A		GROUP B
Some Men of Seville Shaves himself (therefore) Not shaved by barber	**NO CONTRADICTION**	*Some Men of Seville* Does not shave himself (therefore) Shaved by barber
Barber of Seville Shaves himself (therefore) Not shaved by barber	**CONTRADICTION**	*Barber of Seville* Does not shave himself (therefore) Shaved by barber

21. Inequality and the barber

In both cases, group A or B, the barber cannot meet the conditions which define membership of that group because there is an innate contradiction faced by the barber which is not faced by any other member of that group. This is because in both groups, for each of the men of Seville, there are two units involved in the equation: there is the man himself and also the barber. But for the barber there is only one unit, the man himself who is *simultaneously* also the barber. It becomes obvious, therefore, that the barber does not and cannot belong to either group, that membership in either is automatically forbidden and the barber is automatically excluded. Not ejected, since he has never been, and logically could not be, a member of either group. The barber belongs to a third group, of which he is the sole member. In simple trichotomy terms, all the men of Seville are 'Either a or b', whereas the barber is 'Neither a nor b'. To attempt to pressure the barber into being a member of both groups, a and b (shaved by the barber, not shaved by the barber), is to attempt the impossible, and in trichotomy terms this means paradox. So it is the rule that does not exist, not the barber: the rule is impossible of implementation.

Therefore, any re-casting of the Barber paradox must take this circumstance into account. The paradox might now start with, 'Except for the Barber of Seville himself …' However, this would mean that all (apparent) contradiction has now been removed and consequently there would no longer be a paradox.

Bear in mind also that the ideal and condensed version of this paradox would be, 'A man is both shaving himself and not shaving himself, simultaneously'. In this way, all the other bothersome men of Seville would be dispensed with and we could get straight down to the nitty-gritty. But of course, now we immediately perceive that the scenario is impossible since it goes head to head with the law of non-contradiction. But that is the intention of this type of paradox anyway, and usually it is wrapped up in a complex and pretty little scenario such as the Barber, which distracts us from the core issue.

A Meeting with the Barber

'Wait! Wait! Wait! Not so fast! You haven't quite solved it yet!'

You hear the barber calling out to you as he dashes out of his shop to confront you in the street. You are horrified to see that he is clean-shaven. Has the barber somehow shaved while you weren't looking? But you have not lost sight of him for more than a second or two! How could this be?

'Just wait!' I can see what you are thinking. It happens every time. You're not the first, you know! Sometimes I get whole busloads of people gawping through my window, trying to work out who it is that shaves me every morning. Just like you, they allow their imaginations to run riot and they suppose they can see whiskers on my chin, so they prepare themselves for the great revelation. So who does shave me? Well, I shall tell you. You shall be the very first person outside my family to know.'

Wow! This really has been worth the journey, you think to yourself – and has he already offered some sort of clue here?

'The fact is that everyone is wrong. And *you* are wrong. The Barber of Seville *does* exist, as must be apparent, and moreover the rule *does* operate without any problems, as I shall now explain. You see, there is another escape route that no one else has considered.

'When my wife kisses me goodbye in the morning, she does not say, "Goodbye, Barber of Seville." She uses my first name, or says "my love," or "Darling." When I return to my home after a long day, with my poor feet aching for rest, my two little gorgeous children do not rush to the door and greet me with "Barber of Seville! Barber of Seville!" They rush to the door and greet me with "Daddy! Daddy!" – and very nice it is, too! And when I share a bottle of wine with my friends, they do not call me "Barber of Seville" … you get the idea?'

You nod.

'I am the Barber of Seville only between the hours of nine o'clock and six o'clock, and only then when I am in my shop and being paid for my services. The man you see before you is not just the Barber of Seville. Shaving beards and trimming hair is only *one* of my roles or functions as a man. I also function as a husband, a father, a brother, a son, a motorist, a player in my local football team, etc., and in each of these roles I act accordingly.

'But I cannot be all of these things all at the same time and for all people. I also have periods when I am just myself, an ordinary man, doing things that are necessary for my own well-being. So, in the mornings, and before I go to work, I shave myself, as most other ordinary men do. I have always shaved myself, long before I ever trained as a barber. I am a man of Seville who shaves himself and who is therefore not shaved by the Barber of Seville. There is no contradiction here. The Barber of Seville begins work at nine o'clock in the morning. I shave myself at eight o'clock. The Barber of Seville shaves his customers solely on business premises. I shave solely at home, or in a hotel when I am on holiday. The Barber of Seville expects, and receives, payment in return for shaving a customer. I neither expect, nor receive, payment for shaving myself.

'You can see, then, that I am truly shaved by myself and not by the Barber of Seville. The Barber of Seville is not a man, he is but *one function* of the man I am, for I do of course have many other functions, as all people do. I am a barber only for certain periods. I do not shave beards twenty four hours a day. I can, therefore, alternate between being a barber and just an ordinary man who has a personal life. When I shave myself in the morning I am not the Barber of Seville. Thank you for your interest. I really must get ready for my customers now. Goodbye.'

The barber turns and goes, then pauses in his shop doorway.

'Oh, incidentally, did you really think that I could persuade all the men of this town who shave themselves to prove this to me? And did you honestly think I could insist that all those who didn't shave themselves must be shaved by me alone? *I would have to pay them* for the privilege, and with a long queue at my door most of them would be late for work. Or I would have to pay lots of heavies to abduct them and drag them into my shop. It wouldn't have been very long before I was arrested, would it? Did you *really* contemplate that as an option? You did, didn't you?! You must be barking mad! Ha!'

The barber shakes his head, laughs again, and disappears inside his shop. At this very moment, your friend turns the corner and approaches, looking very disappointed.

'Jake the Executioner has fled the village,' she says. 'He couldn't bear the thought of beheading himself whilst simultaneously not beheading himself. All that blood and lack of blood was just too much and not too much for him. Now that he's gone he doesn't have to worry about it any more. I hear that he's moving to Seville. No doubt this will be a ghost town by tomorrow!'

Three Groups, Not Two

The main group, 'men of Seville', is divided not into *two* sub-groups but *three*: those who shave themselves, those who do not shave themselves, and the barber. The barber may be a sub-group with a membership of only one, yet it is nevertheless a sub-group; and potentially, the other sub-groups could be equally small. Size of sub-group is irrelevant.

GROUP A	GROUP C	GROUP B
Men who shave themselves	The barber	Men who do not shave themselves

22. Men of Seville as a group of three

This division into three has been overlooked by those who have previously tried to solve the Barber paradox. It is illogical to create two categories of the self-shaving and the non-self-shaving from the men of Seville and ignore the fact that the barber is also a man of Seville and commands his own category. The obsession with polar opposites and the law of bivalence, or excluded middle, has blinded some analysts to the obvious: that there is a third player in this game. The fact that the barber must be shaved by *someone* does not mean that he must belong either to group A or group B. Indeed, we have seen that he cannot belong to either, since he cannot meet the criteria for membership of either group.

A member of group A is a (man of Seville) who (shaves himself). A member of group B is a (man of Seville) who (does not shave himself). Every member of group A or group B belongs to two categories and two only, as far as this scenario is concerned. The barber, on the other hand, is the *only* man of Seville who is expected to belong to *three* categories, i.e., he is a 1. (man of Seville) who either 2. (shaves himself) or (does not shave himself) *and* is also the 3. (Barber of Seville who shaves others). This is unacceptable and contributes in large measure to the paradox. It is unacceptable because it is wrong.

The reason why the Barber of Seville can, it seems, quite happily shave himself without violating the terms of the paradox rule is exactly as explained above by the barber himself: the Barber of Seville does not exist twenty four hours a day. If he did, then there could be no such satisfaction of the terms of the paradox. He can only shave himself because he is a man of Seville shaving himself as a man of Seville and not the Barber of Seville shaving the Barber of Seville. It is the function of the Barber of Seville to shave, not to be shaved.

A Second Meeting with the Barber

'Are you still at it?!' calls the exasperated barber, as once again he strides over to confront you outside his shop. 'I thought I'd explained everything quite satisfactorily to you and yet here you are still plugging away at it and getting nowhere fast!'

You protest that his explanation sounds great, but that his solution to the problem allows him to belong to only one group – those men who shave themselves – and not the other, those men who are shaved by the barber, and therefore there needs to be further investigation of the reason why.

'On the contrary', says the barber, 'I can, in fact, belong to either group. You see, I did cheat a little bit when I confessed that I always shaved myself before going off to work. Because occasionally – and especially when I've had a drop too much wine the night before – I find that I'm running late and don't have time to shave at home. So, I shave myself when I get to my barber shop, even if it's after nine o'clock.'

'But surely this is violating the rule?' you gasp.

'Not at all', the barber confidently replies, and with one of his little wry smiles. 'I can be a man of Seville and the Barber of Seville at one and the same time! The former role is a passive one, the latter, active. The two are not contradictory! Nor is it particularly unusual to be playing two roles concurrently: The Butcher of Seville buys meat from his own shop. He weighs it, wraps it, and pays for it by placing money in the till for it, just as he does for all his other customers. He allows himself a modest discount, of course, but that is standard practice within the retail industry. The Baker of Seville frequently serves at her own table the bread she has personally baked that very day in her bakery, yet it was also paid for by her – with a little discount, naturally. So there we have it: the traders of Seville treat themselves as customers of Seville when the occasion arises, and I do likewise. If I am shaving on the Barber of Seville's premises then I am acting as a barber and I expect to be paid, to cover my costs for the premises such as business taxes, heating, lighting, and the cost of my materials, such as soap, towels and hot water. I treat myself as a customer and pay for my shave as a normal customer would – minus a tiny discount, certainly. When I shave myself in my capacity as the Barber of Seville it is because I am a man of Seville who has not that morning shaved himself, so it is quite legitimate to do so without violating the terms of the rule. You were correct when you stated that the barber only shaves, he is not shaved.

'You also need to bear in mind that my rule says nothing about timescales. Therefore, in theory, I could alternate between shaving myself as a man of Seville one day and as the Barber of Seville the next. Certainly, this aspect of the rule could be tightened to preclude such goings-on, but this would still not prevent me from shaving myself in one way or another. Further tightening of the rule could force me to work twenty four hours a day to prevent me shaving at home, and could also impose restrictions to prevent me shaving in the barber shop. But if the rule itself insists that I must shave as do all other men of Seville and yet that selfsame rule prevents me from shaving myself at all, then the rule is directly contradicting itself and so has fallen into nonsense and cannot be followed – or even implemented.

'Is that Mad Jake I see in the distance? I'm going inside and locking up! You'd better scarper, too – it's a little bit more than a few whiskers that he likes to lop off! For the very last time – goodbye!'

It would seem, then, that the Barber of Seville *can* exist, and with his rule intact. This is because in one instance he is a member of Group A, those men who shave themselves, and in the other he is a member of Group B, those men who are shaved by the barber. At no time is he a member of both groups simultaneously, and this is the key. Additionally, when he shaves himself or is shaven by the barber, it is as a man of Seville that he is shaved, not as the Barber of Seville. A man can be shaved, but a barber is a *function* of a man, not a man – and functions cannot grow whiskers!

Causes of the Paradox

But what is it that actually causes this paradox, that brings us seemingly to 'both a and b'? The above treatment is legitimate but in some respects just evades the problems and does not fully address what is at the heart of the paradox. So, I should like to examine it a little more, step by step, and without the distinction between a man and the functions of a man.

STEP 1. 'Neither a nor b.' One Group.

Imagine that all the men of Seville have been asked to assemble and stand in a line. You, too, are a man of Seville and so you take your place amongst them. You are all members of just one group, identified by your residency of Seville, and so you are all of a kind with no differences between you. There are no polar opposites.

In terms of the trichotomy of opposites, this group of which you are a member is equivalent to 'Neither a nor b'. In other words, your group is *neutral*. This is the *base* group, from which any other groups will emerge.

STEP 2. 'Either a or b' Two Groups.

Now imagine that your neutral group is to be divided into two, with one group consisting of those men of Seville who shave themselves and the other those men of Seville who do not shave themselves: polar opposites. The self-shavers move over to the left and those who are shaved by someone else move over to the right. Imagine that you are a self-shaver, so you join the group on the left.

As far as the trichotomy is concerned, the men of Seville have now moved to 'Either a or b', and, let us say, you have necessarily joined the 'a' group. However, had you been a man who did not shave himself, then just as easily you could have joined the group on the right. So far, so good. The laws of excluded middle and non-contradiction are operating nicely and there are no problems.

STEP 3. 'Both a and b.' Three Groups.
Imagine now that someone comes along and asks for the Barber of Seville to identify himself. That person is you. In STEP 2 it was unimportant who you were, as such knowledge would have had no effect at all on your membership of either group. However, members of the group on the right are all now to be shaved by *you*. Indeed, you are made aware of a rule that will now operate: The Barber of Seville shaves all those men of Seville who do not shave themselves. You observe that this rule does not in any way impact upon your membership of the 'a' group, since you are *already* a self-shaver.

What you do notice, however, is the effect it would have were you, rather, a member of the opposite group. If as a matter of practical fact you did not shave yourself then this rule would assert that, actually, you *did* shave yourself, which of course is impossible. This being the case, the rule would be out of step with reality. In a contest between rule and reality, reality will always triumph. But, in order to live a quiet life and avoid conflict, let us say that you decide to become a self-shaver again and hence you repair to your former group. Your options have now become limited, but at least there is no hint of paradox.

Unfortunately, your peace is soon to be shattered. You are now informed of an amendment to the rule, as follows: The Barber of Seville shaves all *and only* those men of Seville who do not shave themselves. The *only* is totally unnecessary for your fellow shavers, since they are already captured by other components of the rule. The *only* is exclusively designed to capture *you*. Its effect is devastating. It means that you can no longer shave yourself since you are no longer eligible to do so. You are only permitted to shave yourself if you *do not* shave yourself. This is irrespective of the fact that you are already a self-shaver.

Neutrality and Malsequence

Having already been driven out of one group by this autocratic rule, you now find that its strengthened form has driven you out of the other, also. You can neither shave yourself nor not shave yourself. This is in contrast to the accepted interpretation that you both shave yourself and do not shave yourself. In other words, rather than achieving 'Both a and b', which equates to paradox, what the rule does in fact achieve is 'Neither a nor b', which equates to neutrality (and parallels the Gödel sentence). Therefore, the claim that the barber 'shaves' – in the present tense – 'all and only', is erroneous. He does not and cannot, because the barber himself, as a man of Seville, is unable to be included amongst all the other men of Seville. Therefore, to claim 'all and only', as if this rule is already operational, is false and also a form of *malsequence*, since the rule is attempting to pre-empt the reality, whereas reality must, and does, come first and dictates what is possible as a rule. A rule must first be *formulated* and then *implemented*. In this instance, the rule's formulation and implementation appear to be at work simultaneously. Or perhaps there is even a hint or suggestion that the barber was already operating in this manner before the rule was actually implemented, that the rule was merely catching up with, or formalizing, practices that were already in place.

Yet we have demonstrated that such practices were not in place, nor could they be, whether in the present or the future, since the 'all and only' stipulations forbid them. Such being the case, the declaration that this man 'shaves all and only' is a falsehood, and self-defeating, in the sense that, by tightening up every part of itself to allow of no escape, it manipulates itself out of existence: it cannot put itself into effect.

Removing the present tense and recasting the statement as applicable to the future would be of no avail and would additionally dilute the strength of the paradox, since paradoxes of this type demand that this is happening *now* – present tense. The formulators of a rule must adapt it to what is *possible* and not attempt to fashion reality to meet the impossible requirements of the rule. But of course, to do this would mean the death of the paradox.

The *all* and the *only* having squeezed out the barber, he now stands *between* the two groups. A *third* group has been created by the rule, with the Barber of Seville as its sole member. But we are obsessed by the need to force him into one of the other two, because of our devotion to the excluded middle. Yes indeed, the middle *is* excluded when there are only two groups, but this can no longer apply when there are three. There can be no 'Either a or b or c' option where polar opposites are concerned. Having been forcibly excluded by both groups we are determined to try to force the barber back into one of them. But three into two just will not go.

What is this third group other than the Gödel sentence in another guise, in a different application? It is a third element that cannot possibly belong to the system of two polar opposites and thereby must be external to it and neutral as far as this system is concerned. *It is the attempt to force this neutral group into one or other of the polar opposites that creates the apparent state of paradox.* In terms of the trichotomy of opposites, this third group is 'Neither a nor b'.

Incidentally, if we strip the barber of his title, and call him instead 'a particular man of Seville', this will have the benefit of removing the escape routes that were employed earlier. A barber is a part-time, paid function of a man, whereas our new 'particular man of Seville' may not work set hours and may not be paid for his shaving services. 'A particular man of Seville shaves all and only those men of Seville who do not shave themselves' is far harder to wriggle out of and tightens the paradox. However, bearing in mind that the rules of the paradox cannot exist, such a nicety as this ultimately is pointless.

The Forbidden Third

Let us draw a few conclusions:

1. When a rule forcibly creates a *third* group, all attempts to compel this third group into one of the two polar opposites must end, since the law of excluded middle *no longer applies*. The polar opposites here are, Shave themselves / Do not shave themselves. All the men of Seville must belong to one or other of these groups. So then to introduce a man who, whilst either shaving himself or not shaving himself, additionally *shaves others* is to introduce a third group into the equation. He has an extra duty or function to perform which *no other* man of Seville shares and which is alien to the two polar opposites. I should like to term this additional group the *forbidden third*.

2. Furthermore, the two polar opposites have no interaction with each other, whereas this third group *does* interact with one of the other two groups, and this is where yet more trouble begins to brew. Note also that, of the polar opposites, one of them *must act upon itself* in some way, as in shaving oneself. It is not enough to have, for example, the following polar opposites: Men of Seville who are shaved by their wives / Men of Seville who are not shaved by their wives. To now introduce the barber into this scenario would not give the desired effect: 'The Barber of Seville shaves all and only those men of Seville who are not shaved by their wives'. Who shaves the barber? The answer could be either himself or his wife. No paradox.

3. Casting such a rule in the *present tense* is erroneous and misleading. The rule *is not* operating in such a manner and both logically and practically it *cannot*. In other words, it is *impossible* for such a rule to be implemented. Reality rejects it. There is an element of malsequence at work here, a hidden assumption that the rule is already in operation.

4. The Barber of Seville rule is flawed. It is the rule that cannot exist, not the barber.

5. However, both the rule and the barber *can* exist if we interpret the barber as being but a *function* of a man and not a man, as demonstrated earlier.

6. Remove the barber and substitute 'a particular man' and the approach of 5, above, largely disappears.

If we now produce a simple formula from our results with the Barber of Seville, we should be able to see how the *all* and the *only* individually do not create insurmountable obstacles, but that when applied together they are devastating.

GROUP	FUNCTION	EXAMPLE
a	Acts upon itself	Men who shave themselves
b	Does not act upon itself	Men who do not shave themselves
c	Acts upon group b	The barber: shaves group b

23. The forbidden third formula

		THE BARBER OF SEVILLE SHAVES ALL THOSE MEN OF SEVILLE WHO DO NOT SHAVE THEMSELVES
ALL	a can include c	Possible: Shaves himself/shaves all those who do not shave themselves
	b cannot include c	Impossible: Does not shave himself/does shave himself

		THE BARBER OF SEVILLE SHAVES ONLY THOSE MEN OF SEVILLE WHO DO NOT SHAVE THEMSELVES
ONLY	a cannot include c	Impossible: Shaves himself/does not shave himself
	b can include c	Possible: Does not shave himself/shaves only those who do not shave themselves

		THE BARBER OF SEVILLE SHAVES ALL AND ONLY THOSE MEN OF SEVILLE WHO DO NOT SHAVE THEMSELVES
ALL AND ONLY	a cannot include c	Impossible: c cannot do as the rule stipulates – excluded
	b cannot include c	Impossible: c cannot do as the rule stipulates – excluded

24. The Barber of Seville: all and only

The barber's rule should read: 'Except for himself, the Barber of Seville shaves all those men of Seville who do not shave themselves'.

Secretaries and Unions

Now let us very briefly look at a similar paradox, in order to see if our conclusions are borne out elsewhere. In his excellent book, *A Brief History of the Paradox*, Professor Roy Sorensen relates an apparently true tale from the year 1940. A secretary bemoans the fact that some unions forbid their secretaries membership of their own organization. That is to say, a secretary can be an employee of the union but not a member of the union. She expresses the wish that a union could be formed specifically and solely for these disadvantaged secretaries. However, it is realized that this could not work, since if the new union employs a secretary of its own, then there would be problems regarding her eligibility to become a member of her own organization. Let us express this situation in a familiar form:

'The new union admits to membership all and only those secretaries that are not admitted to membership of the union they work for.' Does the new union admit its own secretary? If it does, it doesn't; if it doesn't, it does. The two groups are:

a. Unions that do admit their secretaries (to membership)
b. Unions that do not admit their secretaries

The third group is:

c. Union that admits all and only the non-admitted secretaries

STEP 1. 'Neither a nor b.' Neutral.	All unions
STEP 2. 'Either a or b.' Possible.	a. Unions that do admit … b. Unions that do not admit …

STEP 3. 'Both a and b.' Impossible.	c. Union that admits all and only the non-admitted …

25. The forbidden third and secretaries

I think it can be appreciated that the 'secretary' paradox does mirror the Barber of Seville in every detail. The third group, c, is illegitimate, since it violates the polarity of two and is introducing a rule that cannot be fully implemented. Innumerable other paradoxes could be devised along the same lines as these, but they would all be guilty of introducing what I have designated the *forbidden third*. The formula for this type of paradox goes something like this: 'A particular element of x acts upon all and only those elements of x that do not act upon themselves'.

By the way, none of the secretaries need worry too much – they can easily apply for membership in one another's already existing unions, so there is no need to create a new one at all!

Therefore, we have offered two solutions to the Barber of Seville paradox. If the distinction between a man and a *function* of a man is accepted, then the rule can apply and no paradox exists.

If, however, this distinction is rejected in order to preserve the paradox, then the *forbidden third* is found to be the culprit that causes it. A third element cannot be fully integrated into a system of two polar opposites, though it may be partially so integrated, as we have seen. But to insist that this third group *fully* participate, while at the same time concocting a rule that totally *excludes* it from so doing, defies logic and common sense. From this perspective, the Barber of Seville rule is self-defeating, and thereby the paradox dissolves and disappears.

(You briefly consider that the discount might undermine the barber's argument a little, catch a glimpse of Mad Jake looming towards you with an enormous axe – and scarper!)

RUSSELL'S PARADOX

Bertrand Russell, the famous English philosopher and mathematician (1872-1970), devised the Barber of Seville paradox as a way of demonstrating in a more popular and entertaining way a far more significant problem that he had encountered, that of the set of all sets which are not members of themselves. This paradox created a huge and insurmountable obstacle for those who were attempting to establish a logical foundation for mathematics.

It is generally agreed that a set (also called a class by some) is a collection of objects or elements, physical or conceptual, that share the same property/characteristic/condition – for example the set of (all) languages, or countries, or teaspoons, or root vegetables.

Thus, the set of all languages would include Polish, Swahili, English, Dutch, Spanish, and so on and so forth. This set of all languages, obviously, would not include itself, since it is a set, not a language. Nor is the set of all countries a member of itself, since you cannot visit it. You are unable to stir your tea with the set of all teaspoons, so this set cannot be a member of itself, either. Nor does the set of all root vegetables contain itself, for you will never come across it in a greengrocer's betwixt the carrots and potatoes.

However, there are sets which do seem to include themselves as members. For example, the set of all sets which contain more than five members does appear to be a member of itself, since it contains more than five members: the set of all fish; the set of all orchids; the set of all bees; the set of all people; the set of all notebooks; the set of all farmers; the set of all geometrical shapes; the set of all bottles; the set of all kites; and so on.

The paradox now arises when we consider the set of all sets that are not members of themselves. Members of this set would include the set of all languages; the set of all countries; the set of all teaspoons; the set of all root vegetables; the set of all geometrical shapes, etc. But what of the set of all sets that are not members of themselves – is this set a member of itself? It cannot be a member of itself, since the property specified is that a set must not be a member of itself. However, that being the case, it seems to be necessary that it *is*, therefore, a member of itself. Remember the Liar: if it is true, it is false; if it is false, it is true. We have an equivalent contradiction here with this set: if it is a member of itself, it is not a member of itself; if it is not a member of itself, it is a member of itself. We have *both a and b* from the trichotomy of opposites.

With the Liar we encountered tralse, a fusion of true and false existing at one and the same time, yet concluded that this resulted in neutrality, not contradiction – but only *if* such a condition could be achieved in the first place, which it could not. Russell's paradox presents us with the same type of challenge, and yet we cannot wriggle out of this dilemma as we did with the Barber of Seville by arguing that this set can alternate between being a member of itself and not being a member of itself. These are full-time sets, not part-time barbers. So where do we go from here?

Russell's response to his own paradox was to create a hierarchy of sets, whereby a set is not permitted to be a member of itself. Such a set may be a member of a set further up in the hierarchy, but this set in turn cannot be a member of itself. Sets therefore belong to different levels and no paradox is generated. There was no logical compulsion behind this arrangement – it was simply that it was found to be practical and allowed mathematicians to proceed with their work without too much anguish or hindrance.

The Principle of Class (or Set) Existence

The principle of class (or set) existence states, 'To every intelligible condition there corresponds a class: its members (if any) are all and only the things that satisfy the condition'.

Within this principle, I believe, lies an error which contributes in large part to the generation of the paradox. On the one hand it is held that a set is nothing other than the collection of items or elements that share a common characteristic or property, and on the other it is held that a set can still exist even when it contains none of these items or elements at all. A distinction is being made between a set and its 'members'. The set apparently precedes or pre-exists its members, and it is this notion that I wish to challenge in my attempt at solving the paradox.

So we find, for example, that the set of all teaspoons is made up of some abstract notion that we might call variously a heading, a title, or a label, which denotes the characteristic of teaspoonness; and also we have all the individual items in the world which possess this characteristic or property – namely, the teaspoons themselves.

However, all these teaspoons, though they are real and do in fact exist in the wider world out there, are not brought together in one place, for very practical reasons – and just as well, since many are undoubtedly lost or buried in landfill, having accidentally been thrown out with the rubbish. No, we prefer *mentally* to assemble all the world's teaspoons and *mentally* to stick them under the appropriate heading, the 'set'. In our minds, then, we happily unite the abstract set with all its concrete members, the heading with all its teaspoons, like a long overdue homecoming, and all is fine and dandy.

But according to current ways of thinking, a set's members are not really all that important or necessary, for a set can still exist and get along quite cheerfully on its own. If I now invent a new set, this will serve as an example of what I mean: The set of all teaspoons on planet Earth in the year five billion years B.C.E. Now, I think I am entitled to be confident that there were no teaspoons at that pre-prehistoric date, but the accepted belief is that just because it has no members is no reason to prohibit the existence of the set. On the contrary, my set satisfies the specification that it should denote an 'intelligible condition' and thereby qualifies as a set. It has an independent, stand-alone existence of its own, regardless of its woeful lack of members. Such a set as this is regarded as a legitimate set, but is simply 'empty', and is referred to as a *null set*, a set with zero members.

The Null Set

It is this notion of a null set that I wish to challenge as a first step in arriving at some kind of solution to Russell's Paradox. Even the set of square circles is regarded as legitimate – null though it may be – simply because square circles are intelligible to us. The fact that square circles do not and logically cannot exist is immaterial because, providing we can think about them, then up will pop a so-called set to confer respectability upon them. Likewise, we can have a set of married bachelors, even though such contradictory gentlemen have never – ever – walked this earth and never – ever – will. This notion that any describable property is sufficient for defining or determining a set is to my mind a very sloppy principle and I shall have more to say about it later.

We must, therefore, ask the question a little more pointedly regarding the true nature of a set, for the sake of clarity: Is a set the heading/title/label that states the 'condition' for membership or is a set the collection of elements that satisfy that condition? It is my contention that the collection of elements *alone* constitutes the set. Yes, the 'label' may be the initial prompt that led us mentally or physically to gather all these elements together, but unless there are such elements to be gathered the label is redundant. If none of the pieces of a jigsaw puzzle has been created, the box that would contain them is useless, valueless: the box is not the jigsaw puzzle, and without a jigsaw puzzle the box is pointless. We can discuss the school class known as 11F and visit the classroom where they are supposedly based, but if there are absolutely no students in that class, 11F, then there is no class 11F. All the talk, all the memos, all the buildings, all the *anything*, are just so much stuff and nonsense that count for nothing at all if there are no students to be discussed, written about, accommodated, etc. The *students* constitute 11F, not anything else. All the rest is without substance. To argue that *potentially* there could be such a jigsaw puzzle or such a class is to miss the point. A set and its 'members' must co-exist, must inhabit the same time-frame.

A so-called empty set is not a set, it is a meaningless, groundless label that labels nothing at all, for there is nothing to label. Certainly we can talk about a square circle as an idea, but we cannot talk about the *set* of square circles since that idea has no actual existence, whether physical or mental. A square circle is nowhere to be found and never will be found. There cannot be a set of the logically impossible, not even an empty set. The idea may exist in some elementary form, but that idea is not the same as the property of squarecircleness. There is no such property. We discussed this when considering the Liar, but it does bear repetition. We cannot conceive of a square circle within a single thought: we need two, first a square and then a circle, and these definitely do not add up to a square circle.

Further, the set of all teaspoons in the year five billion B.C.E. is equally non-existent. Just because it seems imaginatively possible for there to have been teaspoons in that year, but it just so happens that they hadn't yet been invented, does not mean we can, in this instance, wave it through and accept the existence of an empty set. A theoretical set must also be a practical set, otherwise it is an abstract nothingness. The teaspoon did not exist then, so it does not exist now. It may be that mathematicians find the idea of a null set invaluable in their work, in the same way that it is invaluable for them to use negative numbers, but that does not mean that we have to accept that they have an actual existence in the physical world and can go out and find one. A bowl of six apples is far more real than a bowl of minus six apples – and its contents are a great deal tastier!

Let us imagine six identical wooden fruit bowls standing in a row. The first bowl is an apple bowl; the second is an orange bowl; the third is for bananas; the fourth for cherries; the fifth for peaches; number six is for pears. The trouble is that each of these fruit bowls is empty. There is nothing in any of them to suggest what kind of fruit they might contain. Indeed, why must they contain only fruit? Why not nuts or nibbles? Now we fetch some self-adhesive labels and on them write 'Apples', 'Oranges', 'Bananas', etc., and attach one of them to each of the six bowls. However, the bowl for apples, though labelled 'Apples', is still empty and neither contains nor exhibits any morsel or shade of 'appleness' just because of its label, in the same way that its near neighbours fail to contain or exhibit anything resembling 'orangeness' or 'bananaless'. In fact, all the bowls are identical and, but for labels with some squiggly lines drawn upon them, give no indication at all that they are meant to hold fruit. Fruit bowls are not fruit. Labels proclaiming fruit are not fruit. Fruit is fruit.

Sets – in the currently accepted sense of them being separate and distinct from their members – are not as substantial as these fruit bowls; rather, they are more akin to the labels, which in themselves are characterless. The set of married bachelors, the set of all teaspoons in the year five billion B.C.E., and the set of square circles, are all supposedly empty, lacking in members, yet as sets they supposedly still enjoy some form of existence.

But I would argue that these three do not enjoy existence as sets in any way, shape or form. They do, for sure, exist as ideas, as mental constructs, but not as genuine properties and certainly not as sets. Just as the essence of appleness does not reside in the fruit bowl or its label, but in the apples themselves, so the essence of married bachelorness does not reside in the label or the sentence that proclaims it, but in the married bachelors themselves. Yet there are no married bachelors – and, by definition, cannot be – and therefore there is no set of married bachelors, empty or otherwise. A sentence that contains an idea cannot be passed off as a set when it has no actual or logical real-world counterpart. It may exist as an idea, but a property it is not, and therefore a set it can never be.

A set is a collection, not a container. A set is not like a fruit bowl that can either have contents or not have contents, and be unaffected either way. A set does not have 'members', as if those 'members' are incidental to it and ultimately not all that important or necessary to it. Rather, a set, as a collection of elements with a property or characteristic in common, is the *sum total* of all those elements. Furthermore, those elements are *components* of the set, not members of the set. There is no free-standing, separate set to which these elements belong: together, as a whole, these elements comprise the set, *are* the set. What heretofore has been regarded as a set and its members should actually be regarded as one and the same thing. There is no such thing as a set into which its members are put as fruit is put into a bowl. There is just the fruit. The fruit alone constitutes the set and bowls do not even get a look in. If there are no components there is no set – of any kind.

Members versus Components

In the current way of thinking, the set of months of the year has twelve members. But my contention is that, in reality, this set has twelve *components*, each one of which makes a vital contribution to the whole – the year. For that is what a set is: a whole. Whether there are two components or two million, each set constitutes a whole, and none of the components can be considered in isolation. A single month does of course possess its own identity, but when considered as part of a set that identity is subordinated to the contribution it makes to the whole, akin to a piece in a jigsaw puzzle.

Therefore, within the set of months of the year, each component month is not one of twelve, but one twelfth. There is only ever *one* set, *one* collection of elements that share the same property, and each component of that collection is absolutely vital and can be expressed as a fraction of the whole. In considering the twelve months as a collection – a set – the months subsume their individuality. They become fragments of a bigger whole, a bigger picture.

Where does all of this leave us in relation to Russell's Paradox? One key point is this recognition that there is no distinction between set and set membership. The hidden assumption that a set has two separate parts that function differently is one of the fallacies that contribute to the creation of the paradox.

Bear in mind that sets are not natural phenomena. As with propositions, discussed earlier, they are entirely a human construct, artificial, and are not to be found in the fields or the seas of the world or floating around in space. They are a product of the human intellect.

My point is that sets need to be *thought of* – conceived, devised, invented, if you will, and then actually created. They do not lie somewhere out there waiting to be discovered, like mountains or minnows or comets. It is the human consciousness or mind which recognizes that certain elements all share the same property, and in the absence of that mind such a concept as 'property' ceases to exist. We humans alone are responsible for the creation of sets.

Creating a Set

Let us suppose that I wish to create the set of all apples currently in my kitchen. I now scour every corner of my kitchen and discover that there is a total of six apples, so I place them all together in a group on a table. This is my set of apples. But what of significance has changed?

> Pre-set there were six apples.
> Post-set there are six apples.

The number of apples remains exactly the same. Nothing has been added or subtracted. It is only the spatial configuration of these six apples that has altered; that is to say, they are now in closer proximity. However, had I not physically moved the apples but left them exactly where they were, it would be my *mental* configuration that had altered, having mentally located – and mentally 'highlighted' – them. Either way, I will have created a set.

By contrast, if I had been too lazy to get out of my armchair and physically locate all of the apples it *would not* be enough simply to follow common practice and mentally imagine my apples as part of the set, believing it to be immaterial whether there were six or sixty or none at all. It is important to know that there is *at least one* apple in my kitchen, otherwise there can be no set. To suppose that the set of all apples currently in my kitchen can exist even if I have no idea whether or not there are any apples in my kitchen is to commit an error. The existence of the set is entirely dependent upon there being at least one apple in my kitchen. What *does* exist, whether or not there are any apples in my kitchen, is the *property* of appleness. But this property belongs to apples, the apples do not belong to the property. I believe it is the combining of the notions of property and set that has engendered much of the confusion.

A set is a *collection* of elements that share the same *property* and that *collection* can be physical, mental, or both. But a collection there must be. The individual elements – apples, teaspoons, other sets, whatever – must be brought together in some way to create the *whole* that we call a *set*. I believe there are five stages that take place when creating The Set of All Apples Currently in My Kitchen (or indeed, any other set):

1. We state the property (All apples in my kitchen)
2. We identify those items that we need to COLLECT (Locate all the apples in my kitchen)
3. We are now COLLECTING those items (Bringing all apples together in one place)
4. We have now COLLECTED those items (Apples are now all together in a group)
5. We now have a COLLECTION of the specified items and we call this collection a SET (In other words, the task completed, we now *acknowledge* that we have the set of all apples currently in my kitchen)

26. The five-stage creation of a set

There is a similarity here with the life-cycle of a proposition: Stage 4 resembles the verification moment, Stage 5 the verification response. We can see that it is Stage 1 that has been confused with the creation of a set, whereas in reality it is merely the statement of a property that will determine the configuration of the set. *The property comes first, the set comes last.*

Set Self-Membership and Malsequence

Sets are *created*, not pre-existent, and there is no set until this entire process is completed. Before Stage 5 is reached, all we have is a set in the making. Thus a set can *never* be a member of itself, *since it does not exist* until it has progressed through all five stages. It is impossible to collect something that does not yet exist, and *by the time it does exist it is too late to be collected.* Any attempt to bring this about would involve malsequence.

On an abstract level, a set is regarded as a mathematical object. The set of all mathematical objects may well contain all sets, *but not itself*, since it did not exist as a set until all these mathematical objects were brought together as a collection, a set. At the very instant this collection was mentally acknowledged at step 5, it was created and a new set emerged that did not exist prior to this instant. Thus it is logically implicit in every created set that it cannot contain itself. This being the case, it is difficult to see how we can continue to call it the set of all mathematical objects. It is too ill-defined. Perhaps it should be renamed the set of all *currently existing* mathematical objects? Even with this modification, however, there is still the mental temptation to imagine the new set that will be created as already existent! This is not helped by the fact that the word 'set' comes at the beginning of the sentence rather than at the end, which at least suggests to us that it does indeed already exist. (Unwitting malsequence?) It would be better to rework the sentence to produce something along the lines of the following: 'All currently existing mathematical objects collected in a new set'. In this manner we avoid putting the cart before the horse and (unwieldy though the sentence may sound) it more accurately reflects the processes involved. Or perhaps we should just leave things as they are, but be alert to the hidden danger.

The set of all sets with more than five members does not exist at one and the same time as its component sets. It is born later than its colleagues. So it can only be the set of all currently existing sets with more than five members. Or better still, all currently existing sets with more than five members collected in a new set.

The set of all sets (if, indeed, it is possible to have such an infinite set at all, and I do not believe it is, since many of the sets have yet to be created) does not exist at one and the same time as its component sets. It belongs to a later stage. So it can only be the set of all currently existing sets. Or, all currently existing sets collected in a new set.

Actions Not Things

The creation of a set primarily involves *actions*, not things, and sets therefore possess a spatio-temporal dimension. This applies even when we are creating a set purely in mental or abstract terms rather than in the physical world. It is because time and space are so significant in the creation of sets that these factors must be given careful consideration when specifying a new set.

The instant that I remove those apples that constitute 'the set of all apples currently in my kitchen' from my kitchen, is the instant that this set ceases to exist. Being in my kitchen is a part of the set's specified property, so now it cannot exist. What I do still have, of course, is a collection of apples – though not a set, in the particular sense that we are considering the word 'set'. But, if this collection of apples is now in my dining room, it does not instantaneously and automatically now become 'the set of all apples currently in my dining room.' In order for it to become such, I must first have the mental desire to create such a set and then I must determine whether there are any apples in my dining room other than these that are already collected. Even if I do not physically have to seek them out, because I *know* there are no apples in my dining room, I still have to consult my memory for such knowledge. Thus, even though I haven't needed to conduct a search for more apples, I have nonetheless had to go through a form of 'collecting' in order to conclude that the collection of apples just brought in from the kitchen comprises the entire new set.

And what of 'the set of all apples currently in my kitchen'? Well, if we wish to give this fresh consideration we must first of all acknowledge that, should such a set exist, it will be an entirely different one, since there has been a certain lapse of time since the first set of the same name was created. But unless someone else has delivered more apples (or at least one) to my kitchen, or apples have appeared there in some other fashion, there can be no such set. The property exists, yes, but the set does not. Now there is, not a null-set, but, we might say, an unfulfilled or unsatisfied property. (Again, there is a similarity here with that of a statement that doesn't make the grade as a proposition – see the Liar.) Perhaps we could term it a setless-property or a property-without-set? Now, imagine that we hadn't removed our set of apples from the kitchen, but that, as we watched, someone had entered the room, taken one of the six apples, and departed. What of the set now? The answer is that the set no longer exists. If you respond that it is the very same collection of apples, just minus one, I would counter by arguing that the set was created at a particular time and therefore is not entitled to claim immortality. Now that an apple – a component that is fundamental to the whole set – has been removed, the set collapses, just as if one of the six slices that make up a cake had been removed, so that there was no longer a whole cake. The original set had *six* apples, not five, so it cannot possibly be the same set. Certainly, I can instantly replace it with a set of precisely the same name, but I will have been forced also to mentally reconstruct it, even if physically I have not had to do anything at all. A new time, a new collection – a new set.

Solving Russell's Paradox

If logically and practically it is impossible for a set to belong to itself, or be a 'member' of itself, it is thereby redundant to speak about the set of all sets that are not members of themselves, since *all* sets are not members of themselves. This is equivalent to saying that, because it is logically impossible to have a set of all married bachelors it is redundant to refer to the set of all unmarried bachelors – all bachelors *are* unmarried; therefore we can speak only of the set of all bachelors.

Hence we can speak only of the set of all sets. The set of all sets that are not members of themselves = the set of all sets. Yes, you could argue that the set of all apples is not an apple and therefore not a member of itself, and that consequently such non-self-membered sets do exist, but to point it out as if it were a special distinction would be redundant, superfluous, since *all* sets are not members of themselves. Or to put it another way, *no* set can be a member of itself.

Russell's Paradox hereby dissolves. If there is no such thing as set self-membership there can be no generation of the paradox. The paradox's existence relies on the assumption that a set can indeed be a member of itself in certain instances, whereas I believe I have demonstrated that a set cannot be a member of itself in *any* instance. A set of other sets, of whatever kind, is not an exact contemporary of those other sets, and it is principally this failure of understanding that gives rise to the paradox.

This is why I should like to invoke once again the principle of malsequence and cite it as the main malefactor at play in Russell's Paradox, just as it is in the Liar.

Correct: Property → Collection → Set

Incorrect: Property → Set → Collection

The lives of a mother and her daughter may well overlap to a large degree, but there was a time when the daughter was not yet even born; to organize a family gathering, therefore, and invite along the daughter long before there even *is* a daughter would be folly indeed – insanity is surely creeping in. But this is more or less what is happening in Russell's Paradox. This paradox is seating the adult daughter at the family table when she has yet to draw her first baby breath. This is malsequence.

Now it just so happens that Bertrand Russell's hierarchy of sets was more or less the perfect solution to his paradox. It got him out of a tight corner. However, rather than *arbitrarily deciding* that a set cannot be a member of itself, as Russell did, I believe we have *logically demonstrated* that a set cannot have itself as a member. But whereas the stages of Russell's hierarchy are constructed *vertically*, the stages that I am proposing are constructed *horizontally* along a logical timeline, i.e. *sequentially*.

Back to the Barber

It is possible for an item to be a component of multiple sets at one and the same time. A silver spoon, for example, could belong to all of the following sets concurrently:

All spoons	All silver spoons	All teaspoons	All silver teaspoons	All silver items
All cutlery	All kitchen items	All metallic items	All items weighing more than one gram	
All items weighing more than two grams (etc.)	All items longer than one centimetre (etc.)			

And so we could go on. The potential list is infinite, for just a teaspoon. But obviously, for practical reasons, if all or many of these sets were to co-exist, they would have to be mental constructions only. Furthermore, they would have to be constructed on the basis that they could truly be collectable. A non-silver silver teaspoon not only does not exist, it could not exist. I can talk about it, but I cannot in any way conceptualise it. I can place contradictory ideas side by side, but I cannot blend the two, exactly the same as if we were considering square circles, or tralse. In other words, if there is no such property there can be no such set.

So, for the man called the Barber of Seville, it is possible for him to alternate between different sets (shaves himself/does not shave himself), and also to 'belong' to different sets (Barber of Seville/man of Seville) concurrently, while at the same time operating within the rule that he has established.

But as we know, sets are created by human beings, and it is quite possible that the Barber of Seville belongs to many other sets that he has no inkling about. A woman who passes him by in the street every morning may have grouped him with all the people she knows who are well-dressed, or badly-dressed, or happy first thing in the morning, or grumpy first thing in the morning. Sets are – at least initially – private acts of creation. Yet even when shared with others they have to be recreated each time they are to be considered. Whether or not there is a physical grouping of the various components of a set, it requires a mental act for the set once again to reappear, for us to recognize that such a set exists. That is to say the set, The Men of Seville, only exists while you are thinking about it; it does not exist when you are not.

Russell's Paradox and the Forbidden Third

It could seem from the above analysis that the Barber of Seville and Russell's Paradox do not have too many things in common. I have argued that Russell's paradox is caused primarily by *malsequence*, whereas the Barber exhibits only a hint of this, its principal fault being the *forbidden third*. The two solutions are of a different character. However, there do exist obvious parallels between these paradoxes, otherwise Russell would not have created the Barber of

Seville. Therefore, just as I offered two solutions for the Barber in case the first one was deemed unacceptable, I shall offer two for Russell's paradox. In the event that my analysis of set self-membership is rejected I shall now fall back upon the *forbidden third* argument as a means of challenging the paradox, even though my belief is that it never even gets off the ground in the first place. This need only be brief.

Just as the barber became a third group, so would the set of all sets that are not members of themselves become a third group. Therefore, following the same line of reasoning as previously, this set would be forbidden from belonging to either group, or polarity, and neither can it belong to both.

Group	Function	Example
a	Acts upon itself	Sets that are members of themselves
b	Does not act upon itself	Sets that are not members of themselves
c	Acts upon group b	Set that has group b as a member of itself

27. The forbidden third and sets

Once again, group c is the *forbidden third*. It is this group that is impermissible in a duality of polar opposites. Three into two just will not go. Rather than achieving conflict, the paradox merely achieves neutrality, since it is unable to participate in either group a or group b. 'The set of all sets that are not members of themselves' must become (however it might be precisely worded), 'Excluding itself, the set of all sets that are not members of themselves'. Logic does not allow of anything else, since the claim that the paradox makes of itself can have no counterpart in reality and is meaningless in its present form.

Incidentally, the above specification does not need to include *and only those* as did the Barber, since a set can only be composed of one type of member, those having just the one exclusive property. The *all* is sufficient here.

THE CROCODILE'S DILEMMA

A woman is playing with her baby on a riverbank when suddenly a crocodile leaps out of the water and snatches the child. The mother desperately pleads with the crocodile to return her baby to her. The crocodile replies that he will agree to her request, but only if she can correctly predict what he will do: return the baby or eat it.

'If you are right I will return the baby, but if you are wrong I will enjoy a very tasty mid-morning snack!'

The panicking mother agrees with his terms, deliberates for a short while, and then cries, 'You will eat my baby!'

In response, the crocodile drools with pleasure. 'Well, now, I cannot return your baby because if I do you will not have predicted correctly and you were warned that I would eat the baby if you were wrong. Time to cover your eyes, my dear!'

'Not so fast!' shouts the mother. 'You cannot eat my baby, because if you do I shall have predicted accurately, and you did promise to return my baby if such was the case.'

Both mother and crocodile appear to have argued their case correctly and it is this state of affairs that creates the paradox.

The crocodile now has a dilemma. The decision is his and his alone: he has the baby and therefore also has the upper hand. What, logically speaking, should he do? *Is* there anything he can do to break this stalemate? Can the mother do anything else?

As far as the crocodile is concerned, it is irrelevant whether the mother's prediction is right or wrong. If she is right then he cannot return the baby, since that would falsify her prediction that he would eat it. If she is wrong and the crocodile does not eat it, he still cannot return her baby to her, because in this case she will not have honoured her part of the bargain, which was to correctly predict what he would do.

The mother, on the other hand, would argue that it doesn't really matter if she has predicted correctly or incorrectly. If her prediction is correct, the crocodile is obliged to return the baby. If, however, she is wrong, then it is because the child is to be restored to her, and only when the child is back with her can she be said to have predicted falsely what the crocodile would do.

One version of this dilemma can be traced as far back as 5th century B.C.E. Greece. At the heart of the problem, in my opinion, is the failure to make plain exactly what is meant by the word 'predict', and therefore a fog of ambiguity obscures the way out of this seeming dilemma. If prediction is not in any way precisely defined there is the danger that this so-called paradox is really about second-guessing, about the mother and the crocodile pitting their wits against each other, and therefore is not very much about prediction at all, at least as I understand the meaning of the word.

In addition, there is the question of the crocodile's promise, and whether he is entitled to make such a promise in the first place. The Barber of Seville rule appeared impossible to implement, yet we saw that, at least from one perspective, it was indeed legitimate. Has the crocodile made the mother a promise which it is impossible for him to honour, or can he similarly – and logically – pull it off?

Speculative Future Versus Actual Future

First of all, I should like to make a distinction between what I shall call the *speculative* future and the *actual* future. In the speculative future there can exist vicious circularity, self-reference, paradox. The speculative future bears absolutely no relation to what the future will actually be like. Here, everything is up for grabs, everything is seemingly possible, negotiable, changeable. The speculative future is, of course, a function of the mind, of the imagination, and concerns the thoughts that we have regarding future events. These thoughts, speculations, occur prior to some boundary which separates the mental activity from the actual event.

For example, we could speculate about what will happen during the whole of tomorrow, and the boundary which cuts off all further speculation from the actual events, would be the first stroke of midnight tonight. If we were to speculate about what will happen in exactly one minute's time, then the boundary occurs in exactly one minute's time. Speculation regarding the outcome of a particular experiment, test, calculation, observation, will cease at the very moment that the results have been obtained, the abstract and speculative having been displaced by the concrete and actual. The speculative events and the actual events may bear some resemblance one to the other, indeed they may be identical, yet equally they may be totally different. Speculation may accurately predict what will become actual, or it may be wildly off the mark. Whatever its value, the speculative must and will immediately bow out when the actual comes along, for the actual is its superior and trumps everything that is merely speculative. Hope, pray, visualize yourself getting that job at interview tomorrow as much as you like, but all of that will end with absolute finality the moment the decision is conveyed to you.

Below are some of the characteristics of the speculative future and the actual future.

You will note that propositions and facts/falsehoods have been added to the relevant column. Now, propositions may not exhibit all the characteristics indicated, yet they do firmly belong to the speculative. Similarly with facts/falsehoods, yet they in their turn do definitely owe their existence to the actual.

I would like to acknowledge that speculation, as a function of the mind, the imagination, is just as much a part of the real world as anything else. Thoughts are things. To think about something is to participate in the events of the world, and our thoughts, having existed or happened, must take their place as a part of history. So the distinction I am making between the speculative and the actual is about the subjective versus the objective: thinking it and doing it – they occupy different worlds. In the speculative nothing is permanently fixed; there is nothing to which an argument can be anchored, for the speculative future lies solely within the mind, the imagination, and almost anything can happen there.

Speculative Future		**Actual Future**
Speculative		Actual
Abstract		Concrete
Changeable		Fixed
Impermanent		Permanent
Negotiable		Non-negotiable
Subjective		Objective
Conjecture		Fact
Uncertainty		Certainty
Future	Present	Past
Ignorance		Knowledge
Propositions/Predictions		Facts/Falsehoods
Intention		Reality

28. *Speculative future versus actual future*

Tomorrow, for every single one of us, is the speculative future. It may never happen. Most probably it will, if we are of a certain age and in good health, but for others the probability is not as great. Yet who amongst us can guarantee that the future will definitely come? Today we may drop dead of some unforeseen physical complication. We may be run over by a bus – our fault or theirs. A roof tile may drop on our head. Whatever. Even if tomorrow does indeed come, we cannot be certain of the direction it will take or of the incidents it will contain. We will undoubtedly be responsible for many, if not most, of the day's events that we experience, yet we shall not be in control of all of them, nor of every little detail of those that we do author.

However much we may speculate today about how tomorrow will be, at midnight tomorrow, should we still be amongst the living, we shall be able to look back upon the day and see how it *really* was, *actually* was. We shall note that every single instant and incident is now permanently fixed, unchangeable, and is most definitely non-negotiable. It is a granite mountain that cannot be budged. The speculative future has now given way to the actual future, as always it must, and yet no longer can it be designated the actual future, since at the very moment it is encountered it moves from the present into the past and becomes a part of history. Indelible.

Back to the Nasty Crocodile

The Crocodile's Dilemma is rooted firmly in the speculative future, where almost anything goes. It is not connected to the real world 'out there'. If the mother is to make a prediction regarding what the crocodile will do, then that prediction must relate to what the crocodile *actually* does, not what he may or may not decide to do and in whatever way he pleases.

If the crocodile is given the opportunity to modify his intended actions in response to a prediction concerning those actions, then surely this defeats the whole purpose of prediction in the first place? Both the prediction and the action should be non-negotiable. The crocodile should not be permitted to know of the prediction in advance of the action he takes, and if he does know then this is not really a prediction at all.

Action and Intention

This is what should really happen. The mother makes her prediction, but rather than speaking it out loud she writes it down and hands the paper to an impartial adjudicator (yes, I know we are unlikely to come across one strolling along a riverbank, but hey, if a crocodile can talk ... !). The crocodile has absolutely no knowledge of the prediction. This prediction can work in one of two ways. It can be a prediction regarding the crocodile's *actions*, in which case the danger is that the baby may never be returned to the mother, the crocodile having eaten it. Or, the second and more reasonable option is for the crocodile to express his *intention* once the mother has made her prediction (indeed, in the original formulation of this dilemma it is the crocodile's *intention* that is specified). If this intention is spoken aloud in the presence of the mother and the adjudicator, the adjudicator can then compare the verbal intention with the written prediction, which also can be shared with the crocodile. In this manner, both parties are treated with equal fairness

Neither side can then legitimately argue or modify their responses. Here are the four possible outcomes, based on prediction versus intention, followed by the four possible outcomes based on prediction versus action.

PREDICTION VERSUS INTENTION

1. Mother's prediction: Eat baby. Crocodile's intention: Eat baby. Therefore, baby can be returned to its mother. CROCODILE KEEPS HIS PROMISE.
2. Mother's prediction: Eat baby. Crocodile's intention: Return baby. Therefore, baby can be eaten by crocodile. CROCODILE KEEPS HIS PROMISE.
3. Mother's prediction: Return baby. Crocodile's intention: Eat baby. Therefore, baby can be eaten by crocodile. CROCODILE KEEPS HIS PROMISE.
4. Mother's prediction: Return baby. Crocodile's intention: Return baby. Therefore, baby can be returned to its mother. CROCODILE KEEPS HIS PROMISE.

PREDICTION VERSUS ACTION

1. Mother's prediction: Eat baby. Crocodile's action: Eats baby. Therefore, baby cannot be returned to its mother. CROCODILE BREAKS HIS PROMISE.
2. Mother's prediction: Eat baby. Crocodile's action: Returns baby. Therefore, baby has been returned to its mother. CROCODILE BREAKS HIS PROMISE.
3. Mother's prediction: Return baby. Crocodile's action: Eats baby. Therefore, baby cannot be returned to its mother. CROCODILE KEEPS HIS PROMISE.
4. Mother's prediction: Return baby. Crocodile's action: Returns baby. Therefore, baby has been returned to its mother. CROCODILE KEEPS HIS PROMISE.

29. Prediction versus intention/action

It can be seen from the above that the crocodile can *always* keep his promise when it is his *intention* that is operative. In two of the scenarios the crocodile will receive his snack and in the other two the mother will regain her baby. But looked at in reverse, the crocodile remains peckish and the mother becomes distraught.

We can also see that, when the prediction is based on what the crocodile *actually* does, he is obliged to break his promise in two of the scenarios out of the four. This being the case, it is obviously deceitful for the crocodile to make the promise that he does, since logically he cannot in all instances honour it.

What is important to realize is that, irrespective of whether the crocodile's actions are intentional or actual, the mother cannot guarantee to have her baby returned to her if she is reliant on her wits alone. There could be a debate regarding which prediction would optimize her chances of being reunited with her child (and, indeed, which of the crocodile's intentions would optimize his chances of a snack), but I believe this goes beyond the scope of my analysis of this paradox and is not necessary for its solution.

It is clear, then, that the crocodile must specify whether 'what he will do' means his intention or his final action. Only with the former can his promise definitely be kept. If the latter is his choice, then an adjudicator would be of no practical value, and therefore could be dispensed with. Yet even with the former, and in the interests of fair play, the adjudicator should be equipped with a powerful shotgun, just in case the crocodile decides that, upon reflection, the baby would be far more palatable than the logic.

What is also clear is that the mother, in stating her prediction, has crossed decisively from the speculative to the actual, and her prediction is now permanent and non-negotiable. Whilst contemplating her prediction she was firmly in the realm of the speculative where she could vacillate to her heart's content, but having made her statement she has irrevocably crossed the boundary and is unable to change her mind. The crocodile is able to take advantage of this situation, since he has yet to cross the boundary. In compelling him to voice his intentions or to *act* one way or the other, he, too, is forced over the boundary into the territory of the actual.

The Crocodile's Dilemma arises mainly because of the apparent fluidity of the crocodile's response to the mother's prediction. Number one, the crocodile should not be permitted to know the prediction in advance of his own decision and, number two, he really must make such a decision, for that is what the mother is predicting. To disregard these two essentials is to set up a very nice little stalemate that can be labelled a paradox, but which is flawed because of an imbalance within its structure. A card game is in progress and yet one player is being allowed to peek at all of his opponent's cards before he plays his own – surely this is an unfair advantage?

Keeping a Promise

The tussle between the crocodile and the mother is unnecessary. The crocodile has no right to make such a promise, because he may be unable to keep it – whether he is willing or not. For this reason, the mother might be better not to make a prediction at all. Rather, she would do better to quickly pray for divine intervention or, preferably, hurl something big and heavy onto the crocodile's head and then hurriedly snatch her baby back (if the crocodile is talking then hopefully the baby is not already between its jaws!).

The sequence of events should adhere to the following scheme:

Crocodile's promise → Mother's prediction → Crocodile's intention or action → Verification of prediction → Promise kept or broken

That is to say, the crocodile makes his promise; the mother makes her prediction; the crocodile expresses his intention *or* performs his action; the prediction is adjudged true or false; therefore the promise is either kept or broken. Remember that the crocodile can *always* keep his promise if it based solely on his expressed intention, but *cannot* guarantee it if it is based on what he actually does.

Incidentally, there is here more than a passing resemblance to the situation discussed in the Liar. The prediction is equivalent to a proposition, in the sense that it is entirely neutral, neither true nor false. It inhabits the realms of the speculative, where nothing can be fully determined one way or the other. The crocodile's action is equivalent to the testing of a proposition (observation, experiment, calculation, etc.), whereby matters *are* finally settled, fixed, determined. Next follows the equivalent of a verification statement which, exactly as for a proposition, declares the prediction either true or false, right or wrong (yes, there are here also the equivalents of a verification moment and a verification response, but I have omitted these for the sake of simplicity). The great difference between a prediction and a proposition is the obvious one: that the former allegedly describes a circumstance that is yet to be established, while the latter allegedly describes a circumstance that is already established. They may not be close family, but they are definitely first cousins.

The Crocodile and Malsequence

The Crocodile's Dilemma does not adhere to the sequence outlined above. What we see in this paradox is as follows:

Promise → Prediction → Promise kept or broken (No action and no verification)

The second and fifth stages do not sit well in juxtaposition. They do not belong together. It is because this unnatural sequence lacks an action and therefore also verification, that speculation is allowed to flourish. There has been no solidification into a definite true or false, so we fluctuate between the two and all that is achieved is eternal stalemate. This is the unfortunate position of the mother and the crocodile: they are locked into a tussle that logically can never be resolved. The essential neutrality of the prediction is being compromised by the crocodile's illicit knowledge of it – prediction demands action, not speculation. The fifth and final stage of 'Promise kept or broken' has been shifted over the boundary from post-verification territory, where it exclusively belongs, to that of pre-verification, with two stages omitted altogether, and none of this is permissible. Here, once again, we encounter *malsequence*, the pervasive spawn of many a paradox.

So the initial arguments of the crocodile and the mother are inadmissible. A promise occupies pre-verification territory; it is speculative, not actual. Promise, prediction, proposition – they all inhabit this indeterminate realm. It is ridiculous to argue that a true prediction that the crocodile will eat the baby must result in the baby being returned to the mother, because *the baby has been eaten*. It *cannot* be returned. The eaten baby is now actual, while the promise remains in the speculative, and whenever there is a battle between the two it is the actual that will always triumph: the speculative will simply be swept away.

If we remove the malsequence we remove the paradox.

THE UNEXPECTED
EXAMINATION

It is the last lesson on Friday afternoon and you are sitting at your desk in the classroom, finding it very difficult to concentrate and desperately waiting for the weekend to begin. Suddenly, the headteacher enters the room and makes an announcement, as follows:

> 'There will be a maths examination on some school day next week, but you will not know the day of the examination until it actually takes place.'

There are groans all round. As you and your group of friends make your way home, however, one of your number argues that the exam cannot take place on the Friday (the last day) of the following week, for if it had not taken place by the end of Thursday it could then be given only on the Friday and therefore it would no longer be unexpected. Nor, she says, can it be given on the Thursday, for with the last day eliminated, the next to the last day will become the last, so that the previous argument holds, and so on, and so on. Thus your group happily concludes that the examination cannot be given at all and off you go to a doubly enjoyable weekend, since there will be no extra revision for you to do after all.

However, on one day of the following week the headteacher enters the room and asks everyone to get ready to take the unexpected maths examination …

The headteacher has not violated his word, since the

examination was totally unexpected by the students. Yet this state of affairs gives rise to complex logical problems which have been addressed by a succession of logicians over the years, though without a conclusive resolution of the paradox. It is Thomas O'Beirne who, I believe, comes closest, by asserting that a statement regarding a future event can be known to be true by one person (i.e. the headteacher) but not known to be true by anyone else (i.e. the students) until after the event has occurred. O'Beirne's analysis is sound and his conclusions are valid, but only to a certain point and in certain circumstances. I feel that he does not go quite far enough into the ramifications that are exposed by a practical application of it, and which have a bearing on the conclusions he draws. He overlooks many variables that are involved and misses (together with every other analyst, as far as I am aware) a fundamental and pivotal flaw in the formulation of this version of the paradox. I shall proceed, then, with my own analysis.

Within the formulation of the paradox there lies a key idea: *If the examination has not taken place by the end of Thursday …* The valid inference to be drawn from this is that the exam *can* take place on any day, Monday through Thursday, in accordance with the headteacher's rules, and this is indeed the case. If the exam *does* take place on any of these days then there will exist no difficulties and we will lack a paradox – this is found to be implicit within the paradox. Only *when*, and *if*, we reach Thursday evening without an exam is a faulty train of reasoning then brought into effect, one which doubles back on itself and *denies* the feasibility of Monday to Thursday as possible exam days. In practice this is nonsensical, for these first four days *have already passed*. Logically, too, this reasoning is illegitimate: we cannot, as part of an argument, rule out something that is accepted as a fundamental premise of that very same argument. But this is what is being done. To use a familiar figure of speech, the argument is lifting itself up by its own bootstraps.

Five Chocolate Bars and a Hazelnut

I should like to use an analogy in order to make this point a little clearer. Instead of days we shall have chocolate bars, and substitute a hazelnut for the exam. The headteacher makes an equivalent statement regarding these, thus: 'There is a hazelnut in one of the chocolate bars, but you will not know which bar contains the hazelnut before you actually eat it. The chocolate bars are numbered 1 to 5 and must be eaten in that sequence.'

Let us first consider the possible alternatives involved in such a situation.

Scenario 1:

The headteacher allows us to pour melted chocolate into five chocolate bar moulds and then we add a hazelnut to one of them in such a way that it is undetectable. When the bars are solid we wrap and number them from 1 to 5, and we *know* which bar contains the nut. The headteacher then makes his statement, which we *know* cannot be true.

Scenario 2:

The chocolate bars are prepared as above, except that the headteacher numbers them while our back is turned (perhaps there could be an independent observer to ensure the headteacher does not resort to any trickery!). We *know* that one of the bars contains a hazelnut, but not which one (though the headteacher knows). The headteacher makes his statement. We proceed to eat the bars in sequential order. We might anticipate that if the nut is not in either 1, 2, 3 or 4 then it *must* be in 5. If it is found in one of the first four bars then the headteacher's statement is at that point proved true, not before; but if it is not in 1 to 4 then the statement is at that point proved false. *Before* we begin eating bars 1 to 4 we cannot determine whether the statement is true or false. We cannot say in advance that, if we reach the end of bar 4 and no hazelnut has been found, then it cannot be in bar 5, since we personally know it must be – and if we do complete bar 4 without discovering the hazelnut we shall now be obliged to declare that the headteacher's statement was a lie. We have no other choice. Of course, the headteacher, in this scenario, is completely in control of whether his statement is to be proved true or false, since he is completely in control of which bar contains the hazelnut.

Scenario 3:
We have prepared the chocolate bars and ensured that one of them contains a hazelnut, but neither we nor the headteacher knows the nut's location since the bars were randomly shuffled by the independent observer before labelling them 1 to 5. Our position is exactly that of Scenario 2. The headteacher's position is that he does not know whether his statement is true or false at the time that he makes it. Exactly as with us, if the nut is in either 1, 2, 3 or 4 his statement is proved true, but if it is not in any of these it is proved false.

Scenario 4:
The position here is similar to that regarding the unexpected examination. The headteacher places five bars of chocolate before us, labelled 1 to 5, and makes his statement. We have not had anything at all to do with the manufacture of the bars. We do not know which bar – or if any – contains the hazelnut.

Now, we cannot reason in advance that the nut cannot be in *any* of the bars (as with the exam not being possible on any day of the following week) because we can only reach bar 5, *from which this line of reasoning springs,* by eating bars 1, 2, 3 and 4 and finding no nut in any of them. Nor can we, after eating bar 4, reason retrospectively and say that the nut *cannot* be in bars 1 to 4, because they have already been eaten and *no longer exist.* Granted, the nut was not to be discovered in any of them, but this was – *had* to be – determined experimentally, not theoretically. If there *had* been a hazelnut in one of the first four bars then no paradox or problem would exist. As far as we were concerned, whilst eating bars 1 to 4 there did exist the possibility that one of them contained a nut, so we cannot subsequently declare that it was *impossible* for them to have contained one.

Let us review Scenario 2. We know that one of the chocolate bars contains a hazelnut, but we do not know which one. We cannot argue in advance that, if we have eaten bars 1 to 4 and failed to find a nut, therefore the nut cannot be in bar 5 because if it is it will no longer be expected, thereby ruling out bar 5, thence 4 and so on, to eliminate all bars as the location for the nut. Such reasoning would be utter nonsense, since we *know* one of the bars contains the nut. What we would have to do, as we concluded in Scenario 2, would be to declare the headteacher's statement a lie.

The same situation holds in the case of Scenario 4 as for Scenario 2. If we cannot argue away all the chocolate bars when we *know* that one of them contains a hazelnut, but are forced to challenge the veracity of the statement, how are we justified in arguing them all away when we are uncertain as to the hazelnut's existence? If we *knew* it did not exist we could do this, but we do not know. There may or may not be a hazelnut – *this* is all we know for certain.

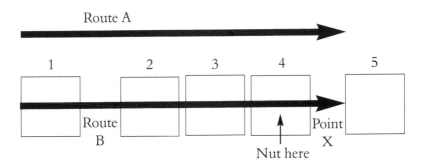

CHOCOLATE BARS

30. Five chocolate bars and a hazelnut

We cannot take theoretical Route A to arrive at Point X, since the nut *may* be in bar 4 (as indicated), and thus to retrospectively eliminate bar 4 (and then 3 and 2 and 1) would be foolish – logic and reason would be totally out of step with actuality. Route A cannot leapfrog 1 to 4 because its very basis *assumes* and *necessitates* that Route B must be travelled – i.e. the chocolate bars 1 to 4 must have been eaten. We therefore can only approach bar 5 at Point X via Route B, eating each bar in turn. *Only then*, if we have reached bar 5 without having discovered a nut, will a problem exist.

The same holds good for the unexpected exam. In the same way that the bars must be eaten in turn, the days *must* be traversed sequentially, Monday through Thursday, otherwise we engender *malsequence*. Route A traverses the days in theory and then eliminates them – this simply cannot be done.

The Last Day Scenario

So, let us review our present position. We have, I believe, successfully exposed the flawed reasoning which ruled out the possibility of an examination being held on any day. Therefore, Monday through Thursday are permissible unexpected exam days. If the exam *is* held on one of these days there will exist no internal conflict with regard to the headteacher's statement and no paradox is generated. However, it is necessary to consider the possibility that the exam might not be given before the end of Thursday, in which case Friday is the only day remaining. Can the exam be given?

If such *is* the present situation, we find that the headteacher is now, in effect, asserting the following: 'There will be an examination on some school day this week. Tomorrow, Friday, is the final day of the school week, and accordingly this exam will be held tomorrow. However, you, the students, will not know the day of the exam before it actually takes place.' Of course, this statement appears absurd. The conditions hereby imposed by the headteacher seem incapable of being met. We naturally might object that the headteacher cannot in one breath make a statement of apparent fact, expecting his students to accept it as such, and then in the next breath negate that statement while still expecting it to stand. The headteacher's statement, on the surface at least, appears to have degenerated into nonsense. The trap is that the students likewise might reach this conclusion and, believing it to be nonsense, be caught off guard by the headteacher who gives them an unexpected exam – the paradox is revived when the students become aware of this danger!

At this juncture I should like to introduce W. V. O. Quine's analysis of paradoxes of this type. Quine says that we must distinguish four cases, and I shall adapt these to the present problem as follows:

(1) There will be an examination tomorrow and I know it now
(2) There will not be an examination tomorrow and I know it now
(3) There will not be an examination tomorrow and I do not know it now
(4) There will be an examination tomorrow and I do not know it now

Quine argues that the latter two alternatives are the open possibilities and that the last one of all would fulfil the conditions of the headteacher's announcement. At first sight this seems like a very tidy solution. However, the danger here, in accepting (4) as the alternative which 'would fulfil' all the conditions of the announcement, is that we may now use it as the basis upon which to further reason that (4) *must* in fact be the case, i.e. that therefore there *must* be an exam tomorrow in order to satisfy the conditions of the announcement. In which case the exam is no longer unexpected – and we are back to square one. I therefore reject Quine's approach.

The 'Last Day Scenario' brings out the very heart of the problem and can stand on its own as an alleged paradox without the need for preceding days of the week. At this point (if not earlier) human psychology steps in – or perhaps more accurately, *might* step in – to muddy the waters somewhat. To my knowledge, no other commentator has attempted an analysis of the situation that might develop should the final day arrive without an exam having been given. So, let us proceed and see if this will yield any valuable insights.

Let us first eliminate from our consideration those students who give no thought to the problem, or are unaware of the announcement, etc., and for whom an exam will indeed be entirely unexpected, even if held on the Friday, and concentrate rather on those students who are using all their reasoning powers in order to resolve the problem satisfactorily.

It is Friday morning. We ask ourselves, 'Is the announcement truthful?' If there is no exam at all today then the announcement was (is) a lie. Can we be certain that the headteacher is dependable, will keep his word (and no amount of evidence in support of his integrity from past experience is sufficient grounds for belief that he will be honest and truthful on this occasion). Thus we have justified doubts. It matters not whether the headteacher definitely does give an exam today, we cannot know *now*, in advance of it, that he will. The situation remains the same even if the headteacher at this very moment is making preparations for the exam and we are observing this activity – we simply cannot be sure that the exam will in fact proceed. Probability may suggest to us that it will, but probability is not certainty and fails to extinguish our doubts. Earlier in this book we distinguished between the speculative future and the actual future: it is the speculative future that torments us now.

We pause for a moment and ask ourselves what might have been in the headteacher's mind when he devised those conditions for an exam. Was *he* fully aware of the logical problems it would create for us, and, if so, did he know what the solution to those problems would or might be? Or, did he devise the exam rules without giving them such deep consideration? If the latter, then he may now realize that he has possibly been thwarted by our reasoning and, believing that we are aware that he is about to hold an exam, and that we are therefore fully expecting it (because it is the last day and so *must* be held), the headteacher might realize that the conditions for giving the exam cannot now be met, and so will cancel it.

Or again, has he always been fully conscious of the problematical situation we are in and proceeds to do ... what?

With these reflections, we recognize there is a tussle between our own thoughts and those of the headteacher. Are we each aware of the other's realization that a difficult situation obtains? Or, is the headteacher unaware himself, and unaware also that we realize there is a problem?

... We could continue like this, to no profitable end. We have reasons why the headteacher might give the exam and reasons why he might not. Rational thought, logical analysis, cannot possibly place us in the mind of the headteacher and apprise us of his true intention.

But what we do finally realize is this. We have no rational grounds for either believing or disbelieving that the exam will go ahead – it is neither fully expected nor fully unexpected. Therefore, if the exam does go ahead, there will be no paradox, only a truthful statement on the part of the headteacher. Similarly, if the exam does not take place, there still will be no paradox, only a false statement on the headteacher's part. If it is objected that such a realization might possibly lead to the argument I used in dismissing Quine's solution, I shall reply by offering a stronger argument where there exists no such danger. And this I shall do now.

I would like to refer again to the conclusion arrived at by O'Beirne, but with which I only partially concurred. He argues that 'a statement about a future event can be known to be true by one person (in this case the headteacher) and not known to be true by the other parties (the students) until after the event has taken place.' This is largely the conclusion we have reached by our own analysis. Nevertheless, O'Beirne's position is not wholly correct. If we apply it to the next variation of the paradox to be considered, that of the 'unexpected egg', we can accept it wholeheartedly (it will even serve for the situation as given in my earlier chocolate bar analogy). But as it stands, with its applicability to the paradox currently under discussion, it fails fully to hit the mark.

Action and Intention

This is because O'Beirne is assuming that, with 'known to be true', the headteacher has absolute control over the future events regarding which he makes a statement, and this is definitely not the case. A person cannot *know* in advance of an intended event that his intention will in fact materialize (we must discount from this argument all 'either/or' possibilities, such as 'Tomorrow I shall be either alive or dead').

The headteacher does not wield absolute control over the future events he announces that he intends to bring about. Playing the part of one of the students again, we see now that the conflict of our thoughts versus the headteacher's thoughts *is not* the only, or even the major, factor in our inability to determine whether an exam will or will not be held. Rather, this honour goes to the countless number of possible variables which fall *outside* the control of the headteacher and which may serve to prevent the exam being given by him and perhaps by anyone else. In asserting that the headteacher can know his statement about a future event to be true, O'Beirne overlooks entirely this stronger point.

Influences of many kinds may conspire against the headteacher's intentions: the school may burn down; the headteacher may fall ill or drop dead; the students may all decide to stay away from school that week; the exam papers may go missing; and so on, and so on. Bearing these possibilities in mind, I, as a student, cannot be convinced *in advance* that the exam will definitely be held. Hence I cannot expect it with one hundred per cent certainty; and hence the exam may proceed in full accord with the headteacher's terms – though *even he* could not know that his statement would in the event prove truthful. In other words, we cannot say of the exam that it *will* go ahead or *must* go ahead – *and neither can the headteacher*.

These unforeseeable circumstances, beyond the headteacher's sphere of control, may intervene to prevent the exam being given – so can we in all honesty afterwards call the statement a lie? Not really. Such statements of intention must always be provisional upon the possible intrusion of external factors which may circumvent the intention. These possible variables inject uncertainty into the very statement itself – that is to say, the headteacher's announcement cannot be either true or false at the time he makes the announcement. If and when the exam is given (not a second before), the announcement will *become* true. But if the exam is not given by the end of Friday, for whatever reason, then obviously it will be proved false.

An exam may have been given with regularity on the last day for thirty years, but there is absolutely *nothing* to assure us that it will be given again this year. There are echoes here of the problem of induction, of scientific method. But within this 'paradox' there are too many potential variables to be able to predict accurately (which is not the same as 'knowing' anyway), and the headteacher is not claiming, and cannot claim, omniscience!

In conclusion, then: neither students *nor* headteacher can *know* before the event that the exam will definitely be given. O'Beirne successfully makes this point in relation to the students, yet fails to recognize that an identical situation obtains in regard to the headteacher. The paradox is generated because we are led to believe that the exam cannot *logically* be held, yet in practice *can* be held, and the ensuing conflict between these two positions appears irresolvable. I believe we have shown that it *is* possible for the exam to be given, both practically and logically, and without violating any of the conditions the announcement imposes – though of course, this can only be known retrospectively. Such being the case, *there is no paradox*, only an announcement/statement which eventually will be proved either true or false: true if the exam goes ahead, false if it does not go ahead by the end of school on Friday.

If, with regard to the chocolate bar analogy, we had devised a Scenario 5 in which neither we nor the headteacher knew whether a hazelnut was contained in one of the bars, we would have a similar (but not identical) situation to that we have discovered here. For a Scenario 5 would have the headteacher blindly making his announcement, not knowing whether it was true or false until a hazelnut was or was not discovered.

THE UNEXPECTED EGG

The paradox of the unexpected egg is similar to that of the unexpected examination, but not identical in the problems it poses. It was devised by Michael Scriven, a professor of logic and philosophy at Indiana University in the United States, and goes as follows.

On a desk there are two small boxes numbered 1 and 2. Your friend tells you that in one of these boxes there is an unexpected egg, unexpected in the sense that you will not be able to deduce in advance of opening the boxes which of the two contains the egg. Further, you can open the boxes only in sequence, first Box 1 and then Box 2. Your friend now asks you to determine which of the two boxes contains the unexpected egg.

You reason that if you open Box 1 and find it empty, the egg must therefore be in Box 2. However, if the egg *must* be in Box 2, then it cannot be unexpected. Consequently, you reach the conclusion that the egg must be in Box 1. But then you are troubled by the realization that if such is the case, the egg once again cannot be unexpected.

It would seem that the dice are loaded from the very beginning with this paradox, since there is the demand that the egg remain an unexpected egg, and any attempt to locate it immediately renders it expected and thereby undermines all the reasoning involved. The egg always remains one jump ahead.

This problem differs from the unexpected examination in two essential features:

1. At the time of the friend's announcement, the egg either *is* inside one of the two boxes or *is not* inside one of the two boxes. This is established in fact *now*, whereas the occurrence or non-

occurrence of the examination remained to be established in the *future*, and this means that we are unable in the analysis of this paradox to make an appeal to 'unforeseeable circumstances.' We find here parallels with the situations outlined in the chocolate bar analogy.

2. The friend either knows the egg's location in one of the two boxes or does not know its location (it could have been placed in 'blind', the boxes shuffled around and finally numbered).

As the person who has to attempt to decide upon the location of the unexpected egg, we cannot be certain that our friend is telling the truth regarding the alleged fact of the egg's location in one of the boxes. Because this is the case, we cannot *with certainty* determine the location of the egg, for we do not *know* that an egg *is* situated in either Box 1 or Box 2.

The paradox skirts over this issue. The friend claims that there definitely *is* an egg in one of the boxes, but this is insufficient. We are being asked to give him the benefit of the doubt, to suspend our own doubts in favour of playing his little game. Yet these doubts are central to the problem posed and cannot readily be dismissed. For, if we *were* able logically to determine the location of the egg, our doubts about it *actually* being in this location would nevertheless undermine our logical conclusions. Logic versus Reality equals No Contest.

We can overcome these questions regarding the friend's honesty, or lack of it, by posing the problem for ourselves. If we dispense with the friend for the moment and personally place an egg in one of the two boxes, 'blind', so that we do not know which box it is in, yet *do* know that it is located in one of them, then we will have removed a major obstacle to our further progress.

So, the situation now is that we have two boxes before us, one of which contains the unexpected egg. Can we logically deduce which box contains the egg? At this point, no. The egg is randomly located, and logic will find this randomness impenetrable. The egg could be in either box, and is, therefore, at this moment, unexpected – perhaps!

If we open Box 1 and find the egg, it will be logically unexpected. But, if we open Box 1 and find it empty, we then will *know most definitely* that the egg is in Box 2, and this being so it *will not* be an unexpected egg. These observations are very simple, very obvious. But where does this leave us? Is there or is there not an unexpected egg in one of the two boxes?

The proper answer to this question is that there *may* be an unexpected egg to be discovered. *Only* may be. That there is an egg in one of the boxes is certain to us. That it is an unexpected egg *is not* certain to us, *until we have opened at least one of the boxes.*

A Random Egg

The reason why, to us, there only *may* be an unexpected egg is because we know the egg to have been located *randomly*. In the original version of this paradox, with the friend making the statement, we are not given the impression that the egg is located randomly, but that it is in a very specific box which will continually defeat all our attempts to identify it.

However, if the friend should try to personally demonstrate the existence of an unexpected egg, what will *he* experience? If he knows the exact location of the egg it will not be unexpected, hence his statement will be false = no paradox. If he *does not* know the egg's location, yet *knows most definitely* that one of the boxes contains an egg, then the unfolding of the situation will be for him exactly as it was for us, i.e. there only *may* be an unexpected egg in one of the boxes. *He is not entitled definitely to assert that there is an unexpected egg in one of the boxes,* as far as his own perspective is concerned.

Is and May Be

What, then, is the difference for us, when the friend asserts that *for us* there is an unexpected egg? The difference is as we noted at the beginning: *we* cannot *know most definitely* whether an egg is located in one of the boxes or not. We do not possess his knowledge regarding this. So that, even after finding Box 1 empty, we cannot *know* that Box 2 contains an egg – we simply cannot be sure that the friend has told the truth.

This is the *only* route whereby the friend can truly assert that there is an unexpected egg. For the friend, as we have seen, there *is not* an unexpected egg, only the possibility that there *may* be such an egg. In the paradox's formulation, the friend asserts that there definitely *is* an unexpected egg in one of the two boxes, as if we should accept his assertion unreservedly. This we cannot do, but *if* we could, then for us there would be, as for him, only the possibility that there *may* be an unexpected egg (this has been demonstrated above), not that there most definitely *is*. Thus the statement he makes may or may not be true, and as to which of these is the case, we cannot know in advance of opening either one or both of the boxes.

When presented with a statement of alleged facts which at first sight seems to yield paradox, we are entitled to ask for substantiation of those alleged facts in the very first instance. It is our ready willingness to place our trust in the veracity of such statements that leads us astray and generates the paradox. If alleged facts are proven to *be* facts, the paradox disappears.

In conclusion, then, and to summarize the above:

(1) If we know the location of the egg then it cannot be unexpected, so the statement is false and there exists no paradox.
(2) If we do not know the exact location of the egg, but do know that it is contained within one of the two boxes, then it cannot

be said that there *is* an unexpected egg, only that there *may* be one. If we open Box 1 and find an egg, the statement is thereby rendered true; but if the egg is found in Box 2 the statement becomes false. Either way, there is no paradox. And because in advance of opening the boxes there only *may* be an unexpected egg, there is no paradox here either.

(3) If we possess none of the knowledge of (1) or (2), which *is* the case for us, then we cannot be at all certain that the statement made to us is true regarding the existence of an egg in one of the boxes – it only *may* be true. This being so, not only can we not logically deduce its location (for it is the equivalent to us of randomness), we cannot even be assured of its actual existence, and therefore the egg remains for us purely hypothetical: we are not only unsure of the egg's location, we are unsure also of the egg's actual existence, and whether or not it is also 'unexpected' is of secondary importance. Hence the statement for us is neither true nor false at the time it is made. If we discover an egg it will be logically unexpected, whether in Box 1 or Box 2, and if we do not discover an egg this, too, will be logically unexpected, for always at the back of our mind there will be the thought that there may or may not be an egg.

We have discovered that, even if we know an egg exists, the conditions of the friend's statement cannot, in *any* instance, be met with 100% certainty in advance of opening the boxes. The friend is trying to impose rules upon us which cannot be realized even by himself.

So here we find – as in the unexpected examination – the statement which gives rise to paradox is the weak link. Both statements give *assertions* of facts, not facts themselves, and contain unwarranted assumptions, and thereby they undermine their at-first-sight seemingly impregnable positions.

ACHILLES AND THE TORTOISE

Twins and a Gateau

You are working in your small café when two men enter. They are tall, powerfully built – and identical. They lumber towards you, knocking over chairs, unsettling your customers, and cast greedy eyes upon all the gastronomic delights beneath the glass counter. Without a word between them they quickly home in on a huge strawberry and cream gateau that was freshly baked this morning.

'Give us that cake!' says the first man, furiously jabbing a forefinger.

'And two big mugs of coffee!' says the second, with a scowl.

'Cut the cake into two. One half each!'

'*Precisely* in half! We're very particular!'

'*Very* particular! Same amount of coffee, too! Do it!'

The café is full, so the two men roughly eject an elderly couple from their seats. The woman grabs her sandwich from the table, utters a profanity, and flees outside with her terrified husband. As the two big men sit, their chairs creak under the strain and the table wobbles under the weight of their elbows. You try to tell yourself that the customer is always right, but the smile you try to project has to do battle with the lump in your throat.

'Certainly, gentlemen,' you eventually say, whilst thinking about furtively phoning the police.

'And if you try phoning the police,' says the first man, 'guess who'll be swallowing that cake all in one go?'

'Wouldn't dream of it!' you lie.

'*Precisely* in half!' shouts the second man. 'We'll be scrutinising the two pieces *very* closely!'

'You don't *dare* give my brother a bigger piece than me!' shouts the first man.

'Give me a smaller piece and you're dog meat!' declares the second.

'They must be *equal!*'

'*Precisely equal!*'

Your café quickly empties of all its other customers as you rummage through every drawer in the back office looking for something with which to measure the gateau. Eventually you find a ruler and, telling yourself not to panic, you hurriedly wash, dry and apply it, but your ruler does not fit the contours of the cake! And is it sufficiently precise anyway? The graduations on the ruler look quite wide. Are they *too* wide for these terrible twins? Might they have brought with them their own, more refined measuring instruments? Will they whip them out of their pockets the moment you set the two cake halves on their table? What if you are a fraction of a millimetre out? The thought of being force-fed an enormous gateau does not appeal to you very much, especially as you have already had breakfast. Your head is in a spin. Your hands are trembling. And you haven't even thought about the coffee yet! Oh, my goodness, what are you going to do?

'The cake! The cake! Where's our #★<★ing cake?!' demands Twin Number One.

'It's just taking a little while to cut it exactly in half,' you feebly reply.

'What's so damn difficult about it?' asks Twin Number Two.

'Well you see, my ruler is straight and the gateau is curved and –'

'Heaven help us!' says Twin Number One as he jumps up from his seat. He grabs a long knife from the counter, wags it in front of your face a few times, enjoys watching you turn green, looks intently at the gateau for a few seconds, and then in one swift movement slices it down the middle.

'Now what's so #★<★ing difficult about that, I ask you?!'

'But ...'

'But nothing! One cake, cut precisely in half. Now plonk them on some plates and get them to us, pronto. Naturally, they'll be free, since I've had to do your #★<★ing job for you!'

'Naturally,' you gulp.

'Call this a café!' laughs Twin Number Two. 'It's a joke! Now hurry up. And those coffees had better be *hot*!'

'Coming right up!'

At the end of your awful day you reflect upon the meaning of the word 'precise' and wonder if the gateau had really been cut in half. The 'half' that the twins settled for seemed to be a lot less precise than they appeared to demand. It most definitely was not as precise as you could eventually have made it, had you been given more time and been free from pressure and intimidation. Besides, some of the gateau – crumbs, cream, fruit – was left behind on the knife that was used to cut it, so how could it be considered cut precisely into two halves when the cake was actually in three places? And if the two halves of the gateau had been carefully weighed, would this have revealed that one twin had received a slightly more substantial piece than the other? Furthermore, just how precise would you have to be in order to be certain that the gateau – or anything else, for that matter – *really was* cut in half? That is, *exactly* in half?

Achilles and the Tortoise

Zeno of Elea lived in Greece in the 5th century B.C.E. and is famed for his paradoxes, the most celebrated of which is that of Achilles and the Tortoise. Achilles, the renowned Greek warrior, is to run a 1 kilometre race against a tortoise, which has been given a 100 metres head start. If we suppose that Achilles runs ten times faster than the tortoise, then by the time that he reaches the tortoise's starting position his rival will have moved on by 10 metres. When Achilles covers this distance the tortoise will be ahead of him by 1 metre. Achilles runs this 1 metre, yet the tortoise is still ahead by one tenth of a metre. When Achilles reaches this point, the tortoise will be one hundredth of a metre further along the course than he is. And so it goes on. However hard Achilles might try, Zeno argued, he can never quite catch the tortoise.

Achilles   Tortoise

31. Achilles and the tortoise

Now of course, Zeno knew very well that Achilles would eventually catch up with and overtake the tortoise to win the race. But his paradox is meant to challenge us to discover what is logically wrong with his argument.

A mathematician would approach the problem as follows:

$$100 + 10 + 1 + 1/10 + 1/100 + 1/1,000 + 1/10,000 +$$
$$1/100,000 + 1/1,000,000, \text{ etc.}$$

However, at around this point he or she will switch from fractions to decimal notation:

$$100 + 10 + 1 + 0{\cdot}1 + 0{\cdot}01 + 0{\cdot}001 + 0{\cdot}0001 + 0{\cdot}00001 +$$
$$0{\cdot}000001 \text{ etc.}$$

This itself can be simplified as $111{\cdot}111111$ etc. Or again, $111{\cdot}\dot{1}$.

But now the mathematician will revert to using fractions and express the distance at which Achilles will be level with the tortoise as precisely 111 $\frac{1}{9}$ metres. A little later on we shall examine the reason for this switch from fractions to decimals and then back again.

Halving a Line

Before we pursue further the problem of Achilles and the tortoise, let us first consider what may be involved in successively halving any line of any length. This is a question that is raised by Zeno in another of his paradoxes, that of the racecourse, and we will find it to be of significance for us here. If we draw a 1 metre line on a sheet of paper, for example, and use a long ruler to locate the $\frac{1}{2}$ metre point, we might be quite content with our measurement and use a pen to indicate this point on the line. If we now divide the second half of the line and mark it as the $\frac{1}{4}$ metre point, we will undoubtedly still be quite happy with our measurement. However, if we continue this process of halving the line to locate the positions of $\frac{1}{8}$ $\frac{1}{16}$ $\frac{1}{32}$ $\frac{1}{64}$ $\frac{1}{128}$ of a metre, and so on, we shall quickly encounter difficulties. We shall find that the graduations on our ruler are just too 'wide' and imprecise for us to be able to progress any further. Any marks that we now draw on the line will begin to overlap those we have already drawn, creating little more than a smudge, and we will find that, from here forward, both the graduations on the ruler and the marks that we draw with our pen, are increasingly broader than the specific distances on the line that we wish to identify. Using these particular tools, we now will have reached a physical limit to our subdivisional ambitions.

We could, of course, resort to using a draughtsman's measuring instruments, or an engineer's, in order to achieve still finer precision, and yet at some rapidly achieved stage we will rub up against the very same problem. Perhaps if we now use a magnifying glass and a needle, then a microscope and a laser beam, we might be able to carry on our work a little longer, but inevitably we will once again and very quickly face an inability to proceed any further. However increasingly delicate and refined our instruments of measurement and marking may be, there will always remain another step that we need to take for yet greater precision, and eventually our tools, and perhaps also our eyesight, will let us down.

Problems with Graduations and Marks

Now, the difficulties that have dogged us thus far are only half the story, because we need to ask whether we can measure even the ½ metre point of the line, let alone any succeeding point. This is because the graduations on the measuring instruments – tiny though they may be – themselves possess dimension, or width, as we have already noted. Therefore, there is the problem of deciding which part of the graduation indicates the true and exact point that we are hoping to measure. In trying to locate the ½ metre point on the line, don't we need to ensure that the precise centre of the graduation matches the precise centre of the line? And how are we to do that? Mark the centre of the graduation with yet another, much narrower graduation? But doesn't that leave us with yet another graduation whose centre also needs to be marked?

½ metre

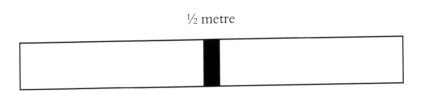

Ruler with a graduation of exaggerated width

There can be no end to our quest for precision. However narrow our graduation may be, it is never so narrow that it cannot be challenged and an even narrower graduation produced. There is never a point at which we can safely stop and declare that the true centre of the 1 metre line has been definitively identified. It simply cannot be done.

As soon as we draw a measured mark on a line and assert that it is the centre of that line we are actually *denying* that line a centre. Why is this? Because a centre is located between two halves, between two distances of precisely equal length, and yet the centre mark itself is *occupying some of the space or area* that belongs to each of the two halves. Hence we do not have two halves, but *three* separate measures. This centre mark is a *third* element on the line that actually *prevents* the production of two halves. There is an obvious parallel here with the *forbidden third* that we identified in the Barber of Seville paradox and Russell's Paradox.

Let us look at this another way. Imagine, if you will, a 1 metre length of wood which we need to cut precisely in half. We mark the centre with a very fine instrument and then begin to saw the wood with a very narrow saw. Unfortunately, however accurate we believed our measurement to be, we are actually destroying the possibility of cutting the length of wood into two halves: the growing pile of sawdust near our feet is evidence of this. Now, we may well be very happy with our two 'halves' of wood because they more than adequately do the job for which they were intended, but that does not disguise the fact that we do not really have two halves. The length of wood is now in *three* parts, not two (if we accept the pile of sawdust as a single unit), and the third part, the sawdust, possesses some of the material that should be attached to the other two if they are to be considered genuine and true halves.

Whatever the type of material to be cut, whatever the type of tool that does the cutting, there is no getting around the fact that two genuine halves can never be obtained. So it is even if we do not actually cut the length of wood (or whatever) but merely mark its centre point: the mark becomes the third element and thereby denies the possibility of two halves being created. *Beneath* that mark may lie the true centre point, but *where is it*?

Of course, in the real world we need centre marks, graduations and so on, and they work very well indeed for us. But they really offer only *approximations*, since an exact ½, ¼, ⅓, etc. is unachievable. Yes, when we look at a line we can judge whereabouts these ½, ¼, ⅓ points are approximately located, but we can never pin them down precisely, since there is always a greater degree of accuracy to which we could take them. It is similar to a camera in space that zooms in on planet Earth, then a country, a region, a city, a street, a house, a room, a person, the gun they are holding, and finally stares down the barrel to view a bullet approaching us in slow motion. In our relentless pursuit of precision we also can zoom in on the mark we have drawn on a line, until the ink becomes greatly magnified, so that eventually we are at the molecular level, then the atomic, then the subatomic, and eventually find ourselves trying to measure the space between a nucleus and an electron or whatever else may be going on in the quantum world. Where do we end? *Can* we ever end?

When it is asked, 'How long is the coastline of Britain?' there comes the reply, 'To what degree of precision do you wish to measure it?' Ordnance Survey, the mapping authority for the United Kingdom, records the length of the coastline of England, Scotland and Wales combined as 11,073 miles (17,820 km). However, this length will increase significantly if we wish to include greater detail in a map of larger scale. For example, should we measure every individual rock on the coast? Every fissure in every rock? Every tiny individual bump inside every fissure? Again, the process could be never-ending. Britain's coastline could be found to be infinitely long.

Hidden in the Nebulous

The most celebrated number in mathematics is π, or pi, which denotes the length of the circumference of a circle divided by the length of its diameter. As a fraction it is commonly expressed as $^{22}/_7$, though this is somewhat inaccurate as a true measurement. In decimal notation it is usually expressed to three places, as 3·142, which again is far from being precise. The exact value of π can never be determined, though its first twenty decimal places are 3·14159265358979323846. With the aid of modern computers, it can now be calculated to billions, perhaps trillions, of places. However, as with the speed of light which can be increasingly approached yet never reached, so, too, can the value of π be increasingly approached, yet never reached. This is because numbers are rigid; they lack the fluidity and subtlety that are required to capture π. π lies beyond and between number. It is, perhaps, hidden in the nebulous: a place that transcends the physical.

Similarly, the division and successive subdivisions of a line (or indeed any object) are beyond the capacity of our instruments of measurement. We can only increasingly approach, say, a half, a quarter, a third – we can never actually arrive at them. Furthermore, any attempt to locate any such fraction by employing some kind of mark or graduation, will serve only to obscure it, since the mark itself possesses dimension. A true half, a true quarter, a true third, may indeed exist, but just like π they are eternally elusive on a physical level. Though we know whereabouts on a line to look for them, we can never actually find them. All we can ever achieve, at best, are closer and closer approximations of them. They, too, are hidden in the nebulous.

Perhaps if we discount the width of the graduation and designate its left hand edge as the ½ metre point, this will give us greater precision? After all, this is how some degree of accuracy is achieved on an athletics track. The standard width of a starting line on a modern running track is 5cm and no part of a competitor's body may transgress the farthest edge of this white line until the starting pistol has been fired. However, the same difficulties of precision will manifest themselves when such a white line is painted on a track. Where does the edge of the line begin and end? When we zoom in on an edge we will discover it to be very irregular and in reality not too straight at all, with bits jutting in and out all along its length, and at the microscopic level this will become even more problematical. So the question will be, where does the track actually, truly begin and end? Similarly, we can ask of our 1 metre line, where does it actually, truly begin and end? It is not just the centre point and other points on the line that raise difficulties for us, it is also the two ends of the line. If we cannot be 100% certain about where a line actually begins and ends, how can we possibly hope to achieve any kind of accuracy when using them as our starting points to measure other points on the line?

Approximations are all that we can obtain and human beings have learned to live with them. The twins were happy enough with their 'halves' of cake that were not really halves at all. Had they been as fussy and particular as we at first believed them to be, then after much measuring and weighing they may have received more-equal portions than they actually did, but those portions still would not have been equal enough. In our quest for ever greater precision we would need to be measuring and weighing the cake long after it had decomposed and disappeared.

Earlier, we spoke of the switch from fractions to decimals and then back to fractions again. This is done because the extensive use of fractions would soon become far too unwieldy, whereas decimals are far more economical. However, $111 \cdot 11111$ recurring leaves an infinite trail of 1s, giving the impression that Achilles never can catch up with and overtake the tortoise. Decimals, which deal in tenths, cannot adequately express certain numerical values, and hence the switch back to fractions to demonstrate that, actually, Achilles *can* and *does* draw level with the tortoise at precisely 111⅑ metres. All of the 1s of this infinite series converge upon this fraction. It is perhaps easier to grasp this if we times the ·11111 recurring by 9 and observe that it is ·99999 recurring, in other words, always approaching 1. Therefore, ·11111 is always approaching ⅑, but can never quite reach it. But whether we utilize an infinite series of 1s or ⅑, the reality is that, while they may work perfectly adequately for all of our everyday purposes, neither of them can be precisely defined.

Back to the Racetrack

So, where does all of this leave us in regard to our race between Achilles and the tortoise? Well, Zeno's entire argument is predicated upon the ability to chop up the racetrack into precisely measured units. In the early stages of the race this is not too much of an issue, since it is visibly and readily evident that the tortoise is ahead of Achilles at various measuring points and we are not really focusing upon the ¹⁄₁₀ fractions involved. However, these fractions become critical when Achilles is on the verge of catching up with the tortoise. Yet as we have seen, it is impossible to precisely locate or identify these ¹⁄₁₀ distances, and especially so at the level of the infinitesimal. This being the case, the argument that Achilles can never catch the tortoise because it will always be ¹⁄₁₀ ahead of him fails. It fails, not solely because when we get to the very tiny values of a tenth of a tenth of a tenth, etc., they begin to merge one into the other and are indistinguishable, but because they are unobtainable in the first place. In other words, the tortoise is never ¹⁄₁₀ ahead of Achilles because – at least on a physical, measurable level – ¹⁄₁₀ *of one item* does not exist.

It is true that Zeno never actually mentions tenths but speaks about 'points', that whenever Achilles reaches the point at which the tortoise was a moment ago the tortoise will have moved ahead and reached another point, and so on, and so on. Yet the same reasoning applies, since these points, on a racetrack or a line, must themselves possess dimension. Whatever mathematicians may aver about points having no dimension, or however useful these abstract points may be in their calculations and so on, in the natural, physical world, such points do not exist. This is a real-world racetrack having real-world dimension (even though we cannot achieve absolute precision regarding it) and it is erroneous and incongruous therefore to superimpose upon it abstract points which themselves *lack* dimension. It is a bit too much like having your cake and eating it. If a point really does exist then it ought to be detectable. This is a case of the abstract versus the empirical. Show me a point and I will show you that it possesses dimension. If you cannot show me it then I will question its very existence.

When Achilles is about to catch up with the tortoise, at the 111⅑ point, the 'edges' of their physical bodies begin to blur. That is to say, at a microscopic or subatomic level there exists a fuzziness, so that it is impossible to determine where one of them ends and the other begins. This ⅑ of a metre is very large and clunky. It is acceptable as far as any spectators are concerned, but is thoroughly inadequate if we wish to observe what is happening at a much smaller level. However, were we to position the very best of cameras at this point on the side of the racetrack and use it to record the instant of the catch-up, we still would have insufficient detail to satisfy us regarding what is really happening at that moment. There are athletes who are deemed to have achieved a dead heat in a photo finish because, even at 3,000 frames per second, it is impossible to separate the two in relation to the finish line. The cameras are simply not up to the job of capturing the very, very small. It is the very, very small that Zeno has managed to befuddle us with, but at this level it is difficult to be certain where space ends and an object begins and at what point Achilles and the tortoise begin to overlap.

Another factor in the paradox of Achilles and the tortoise is that of time. The argument goes that because there are an infinite number of points that Achilles has to traverse, this is equivalent to an infinite number of tasks that he has to perform, and these tasks cannot be completed in a finite period of time. However, since my contention is that there are no dimensionless points at all on the racetrack, this argument does not hold.

In summary:

1. At a macroscopic level (big enough to be visible to the naked eye) we can determine where a line, a track, or whatever, begins and ends, but at a microscopic level we cannot. Therefore, when dealing with distances which become infinitely small, from which point do we begin our measuring, and how accurate is that point anyway?

2. Measuring instruments, however delicate and refined, can never be accurate enough.

3. Any marks or graduations that are used to identify a distance or location themselves possess dimension and therefore will to some degree mask or obscure the desired measurement. Indeed, just one graduation, of whatever width, will have merged a multitude of other, tinier, fractions that could be measured and which actually should be separate. All of these become 'smudged' together.

4. A precise measurement is unachievable, since it can always be taken to a further degree of accuracy. All that can be achieved are approximations, which are more than acceptable in our macroscopic world.

5. Since a precise measurement can never be obtained, the tortoise can never be at a precise place on the racetrack. This being the case, the assertion that the tortoise will always be at some point farther ahead of Achilles does not hold.

6. A line is continuous and cannot be chopped up into discrete units of a specified length. When it seems that it can, in reality only approximations have been achieved.

Zeno's other Paradoxes

The paradox of the racecourse (or dichotomy) bases its arguments upon the successive halving of a line, stating that because a runner must first run half the course, then a further half of the remaining course, then another half, and so on, he can never actually complete it, because the series ½, ¼, ⅛, ¹⁄₁₆, ¹⁄₃₂, etc., is infinitely long. I believe that the arguments I have already advanced apply to this paradox also.

Similarly with the argument that a runner can never actually begin his race, since before he can reach the halfway point he must first reach one quarter of the distance, one eighth, one sixteenth, and so on, ad infinitum.

With the paradox of the Arrow, Zeno argues that an arrow in flight must always be at rest. This is because at each instant during its flight the arrow is motionless. An instant is conceived as being a point in time which itself has no duration but is totally static, with no beginning, middle or end. The arrow cannot move from one position to another during this instant, otherwise the instant would be manifesting duration, which it lacks. Therefore, since the arrow is at rest at every instant, and there exists an infinity of instants, how can it be in flight? How does the arrow get from being at rest in one instant to being at rest in a later instant if it is absolutely unable to move from one to the other?

Nicholas Falletta argues that a photograph of a moving beach ball cannot be distinguished from that of a stationary beach ball, in support of the view that in fact we can obtain 'instants.' Perhaps to the naked eye these two photographs may not reveal any significant difference. However, were the same camera to capture the beach ball travelling at a far greater speed, say 1,000 miles per hour, then the photograph would be very fuzzy, indicating that the ball was indeed in motion. Actually, rather than an identifiable beach ball, all that the camera would record is a long streak of colour. There is no camera in existence, nor will there ever be, that is capable of recording a duration-free instant. However minute the camera's exposure time may be, it is still measurable (approximately!). In a paper published in 2003, Peter Lyn argues that there are no such instants, that they are abstract notions that do not exist and cannot be achieved in our physical world, and I would concur with his views.

Instants, like points, exist in the mind, not in practice. Just as I argued that a square circle can be contemplated but not conceived, thought about but not brought into being even conceptually, so too I would argue that points and instants are really products of the imagination that have no counterpart in the real world. When mathematicians connect one 'dimensionless' point to another using a straight line, they are assigning dimension to those points, for the simple reason that the line itself has dimension (width). However narrow the line is drawn it is always detectable and measurable. If the line is made as 'dimensionless' as a point it would disappear and cease to be a line.

PREMONITIONS

Too quick to believe and you're easy to deceive;
Too quick to deny and the truth may pass you by.

In 1966, as a twelve-year-old, I watched terrible scenes emerging from the mining village of Aberfan in South Wales, on our black-and-white television set. I cannot remember the detail of what I saw, only the impression that it left upon me. At 9.15 am on Friday, 21ˢᵗ October, an enormous slag heap slid at great speed down a hillside and engulfed about twenty houses and the back of Pantglas Junior School. The pupils had only just returned from their assembly, at which they had sung *All Things Bright and Beautiful*. A total of 144 people died that morning, including 116 children and five of their teachers.

It was perhaps a dozen years later that I first learned how one of the schoolgirl victims, Eryl Mai Jones, seemingly had a premonition of the disaster. On 20ᵗʰ October she told her mother that she had something important to tell her. 'Mummy, I'm not afraid to die,' she said. Her mother dismissed talk of death at such a young age and offered her daughter a lollipop, which she refused. 'Mummy, let me tell you about my dream last night,' said the girl. 'Darling, I've no time now. Tell me again later,' her mother replied. 'No, Mummy, you must listen. I dreamt I went to school and there was no school there. Something black had come down all over it.' The ten-year-old was killed the very next morning.

I don't know if Eryl Mai Jones did indeed have a genuine premonition of what was to come. It is said that many people had voiced their concerns about the slag heaps built upon the hillside, so it could well be that the girl picked up on this and that the dream's proximity to the event was purely coincidental. I once dreamt of an acqaintance whom I hadn't seen for perhaps two years, and two days later I bumped into that person again. It would be easy to attribute some supernatural power to my dream and to assert that the two events were linked. However, a later dream which featured the same person was not followed by a similar meeting, and our next meeting was not preceded by a dream at all. So coincidence is very likely the cause of many apparently prophetic dreams, and indeed, recent research tends to reinforce this view.

That said, however, there are very many other instances of alleged premonition. Can they all be ascribed to coincidence, or might some of them have a measure of authentic prophetic content? Shouldn't we at the very least consider them, investigate them? I do know there are some of a scientific persuasion who would dismiss such investigation with a sneer of contempt, and some of religious affiliation who would attack it as a collaboration with the devil. Such attitudes astonish and puzzle me. I believe that in the quest for knowledge and truth we must be open-minded and objective and do our best to get to the bottom of such matters. As far as I am here concerned, I am attempting to apply reason and logic to the issue, which to me seems reasonable and logical.

But there is a problem. What exactly do we mean by 'premonition'? If we mean foreknowledge of the future, then we mean foreknowledge of an event or events that *must* happen, otherwise it is not the future. If we mean foreknowledge of a potential future – the possible or probable – then we are talking about foreknowledge of events that only *may* happen, since that future isn't irrevocably fixed. In the latter case, if such premonitions do occur, we can at least breathe a metaphorical sigh of relief, since the future would appear to be to some extent malleable. In the former case, however, such premonition of an event would mean that absolutely no kind of human intervention could prevent it from happening. Should the future be rigidly inflexible in this way, then it would give rise to a very uncomfortable paradox.

If every fine detail of the future is already 'out there' somewhere, human beings are in deep trouble. It would mean that the free-will we so greatly cherish is nothing more than an illusion and that we are destined to exercise it in a pre-determined way. On the one hand there appears to be strong evidence for premonitions. On the other there appears to be strong evidence for human free-will. The two are apparently mutually incompatible. Therein lies the paradox: if we have genuine free-will there can be no genuine premonition; if we have genuine premonition there can be no genuine free-will. Yet we appear to have them both.

But do we? What is *really* going on? I cannot pretend to know the answer to these questions, that I have got it all sorted out and neatly packaged in my mind. What I do hope to achieve in the following pages is a little more clarity with regard to the problem. I shall also offer my speculations as to how the two opposing camps – free-will versus premonition of the future – can be amicably reconciled. It will require a leap of the imagination and a willingness to venture where science has hardly yet trodden, and indeed where many scientists may not wish to tread, but nevertheless I believe the journey is well worth the making. I am offering an hypothesis, as scientists do, and there is nothing wrong in that.

It may well be that Eryl Mai Jones really did have a premonition, yet that is not quite the same as saying she saw the future. Being too quick to believe in premonitions and other allegedly psychic phenomena can leave us exposed to all manner of deceptions, whether through the agency of other people or by our own – dare I say it – gullibility. Alternatively, being too quick to deny the existence of phenomena that lie outside our own experience or scientific model or religious doctrine may well deprive us of truths to which we are blinded by our arrogance. I shall opt for the middle path, between the two, which to me seems a measured and very sensible route. For the purposes of this analysis, whether it be so in fact or not, I shall assume that the premonitions I discuss are all genuine.

Three Possible Types of Premonition

I believe there are three possible types of premonition.

PREMONITION TYPE 1	Event *has* happened
PREMONITION TYPE 2	Event *may* happen
PREMONITION TYPE 3	Event *must* happen

33. Three possible types of premonition

Let us look at each premonition type in turn and discuss exactly what is meant by them, and later on I shall examine how they might apply to Eryl Mai Jones's experience.

Premonition Type 1: Event has happened

At first glance it could seem that I have made a laughable mistake. How is it possible to have a premonition of an event that has already taken place? There does appear to be a contradiction, I would agree; and yet, there are tests performed which aim to measure precognitive ability that are doing nothing of the sort – they are actually attempting to perceive the past, or the present, and *not* the future.

Let me offer some examples. If there is a shuffled pack of playing cards on a desk and a person (the *percipient*) is asked to predict which card is on the top of the pack, which card is next, and next, and so on, then however successful that person may be in identifying the cards, it is certainly not premonition that is taking place, since the order of the cards is *already established before he begins the experiment.* This person would be uncovering the past, or the present, as the cards are turned over, not revealing the future. *Retro*-cognition? Or something else?

A more effective procedure in using playing cards to test for precognitive ability would be to have the percipient predict which card will be on top of the deck in advance of it being thoroughly shuffled. Then another prediction is made, and the pack is again thoroughly shuffled, and so on. In this way, there would be no possibility of 'predicting' what already is established or partially established. Further, it would be preferable to have the card deck shuffled by several individuals following each prediction, in order to maximise the randomness of the procedure. The 'free-will' element of the shuffling by several individuals, who should be permitted to shuffle for as long as they wish, is to be preferred over the use of a machine, which is subject to physical laws and possible subtle mental influences, for all its supposed suitability for generating random outcomes.

It could be that, in the case of randomly generated computer images, a pure guess is made and then the mind is influencing the selection of the subsequent image, so that it is not precognition that is at work, but telekinesis, the movement of an object by thought or will-power. However, introduce the human element in place of the mechanical/electronic, and such influence over selection is perhaps less likely to occur, though cannot be entirely dismissed. Granted, telekinesis may sound just as – if not more – improbable than premonition to many of us, yet in tests it is imperative to take into consideration all unwelcome possibilities and factor them out. That said, I have to say that I am not impressed by some of the statistical evidence advanced in favour of precognition: a measly few percentage points above what is considered chance does not inspire very much confidence.

In his book, *The Power of Premonitions*, Larry Dossey offers the following scenario as a typical example of precognition: 'An individual may slow down before rounding a curve for some reason that is not apparent, only to find a few seconds later that the road ahead is blocked by an accident.' To my mind, this is not an example of precognition at all, though it could be an example of intuition. Yes, the mechanism whereby an accident is intuited may seem just as improbable to many and would certainly constitute something of a mystery to much of present-day science, yet the mechanism whereby an event is foreknown would be even more problematic. My purpose here is to offer a possible solution to the paradox of premonition versus free-will, not speculate upon the ins and outs of alleged psychic abilities, though in doing so I shall be obliged to stray into that territory. For most people, however, intuition would be a far more acceptable and understandable phenomenon than premonition.

I would argue that the motorist approaching the bend in the road slows down because he has an intuition regarding an event that has *already* happened or is *currently* happening – it is just that he is not as yet able to perceive it with his physical senses. The curve in the road masks the accident from the motorist's vision: had the road been straight he would have received *sensory* information regarding the accident rather than *extra-sensory* information. The accident may well be in the motorist's *visual* future, but at the instant he is made aware of it the event has already occurred. A more impressive example of such a scenario would be if the motorist received warning of an accident that is to occur around the same curve in the road one week from now. This would place the accident most definitely in everyone's future. Besides, if he had been more finely attuned to his 'premonition', perhaps it would have indicated to him that this accident had already taken place.

Perhaps we might agree, then, that Premonition Type 1 is not a genuine premonition, since it offers not *fore*knowledge, but knowledge of the past or present. Such being the case, there is no paradox generated here.

Premonition Type 2: Event may happen

I would contend that a future event that is allegedly foreseen is in reality already taking shape in some form or other at the very moment that it is foreseen. If members of your family are planning a surprise party for your birthday and you get wind of it, it would no longer be a surprise party. A similar process is, I believe, the case with premonitions: a person is 'getting wind of' a potential future event, the components of which are currently being assembled. By 'assembled' I do not necessarily mean that there is human input, though there could be; it could simply be that natural laws of the universe are running their course and in so doing they give rise to certain indicators which suggest a possible or probable outcome. But that outcome has no current existence – it is solely a *potential* outcome which may or may not manifest, and is not already 'out there', just waiting to be encountered. Human intervention – whether conscious or unconscious – may play a part in thwarting its manifestation, or in changing its direction. Natural events may have a similar impact. For example, your surprise birthday party that you already know about may actually be cancelled at the last minute due to someone deliberately harming you, or due to a death in the family – there are endless possibilities.

Dossey opens his book with a case of premonition from the files of the Rhine Research Center in the USA, and I should like to retell this story briefly as it illustrates precisely the points I am attempting to make.

At 2.30 a.m. a woman called Amanda awoke from a nightmare

in which a chandelier fell upon and killed her baby daughter who was sleeping in the nursery. In the dream, Amanda noted that a clock read 4.35 a.m. and that a storm was raging outside. When she told her husband about her disturbing dream he laughed, said it was silly, and told his wife to go back to sleep. But fear prompted her instead to fetch the child and put it in bed with her. The weather was calm. Two hours later she and her husband were awakened by a violent noise from the next room. They rushed to investigate and found that the chandelier had plummeted onto the baby's crib and crushed it. A clock in the room read 4.35 a.m. and outside a fierce storm was in progress.

This premonition at first sight does seem rather impressive. And yet, elements of it are not all that remarkable. A weather forecaster might well be able to accurately predict that a storm would be blowing at that particular time in that particular area based on the data that he already has to hand a few hours in advance of this time. Had Amanda already seen or heard the weather forecast for that night? We are not informed. There does exist the possibility that she could have applied this information in her dream. But if she had not seen the forecast, how then could such information be obtained purely by intuitive methods? We shall speculate upon this later. Yet obviously, this is but a secondary issue.

The main issue is the remarkable premonition regarding the falling chandelier. I would venture, however, that at 4.35 a.m. the chandelier has not suddenly and inexplicably broken free from its fixing on the ceiling, but rather, there has been progressive wear and tear which has reached such a critical point of weakness that failure of the fixing (or ceiling or some other relevant component) is imminent. In fact, based on the weight of the chandelier and the type and rate of deterioration of the fixing or whatever was the main cause of the failure (we are not told, and to my mind such information is vital), it would very likely be possible to predict that in just over two hours' time when it is 4.35 a.m. and a storm is underway the fixing (let us say) will finally give way and the whole lot will come crashing down. If the child is in its crib at that time, then it is inevitable that it will either be killed or severely injured.

But the baby *was not* harmed. Hence the premonition was not of the future, since that future did not occur as it was 'seen' to do. If the premonition was truly of the future, then Amanda would in some way have been constrained from saving her baby and her baby would have, *must have*, been killed. In fact, what Amanda had seen in her dream was a potential future – what *may* happen, not what *must* happen. Amanda alternatively could have moved the crib to another part of the nursery to thwart the realization of the premonition, though the chandelier would still have fallen and the baby might still have been in some danger from flying glass. Or she could have removed the chandelier from the ceiling, thereby neutralising the premonition altogether.

Premonition Type 3: Event must happen

Are there any events that *must* happen? I would argue that there are, but with a particular caveat. For example, I would assert that the sun will rise again tomorrow, that the moon will be in a precise location at 3.00 o'clock tomorrow afternoon, that gravity will continue to glue us all to planet Earth next Tuesday unless we use a machine to overcome it. But although these examples appear to be scientific certainties that we cannot argue with, there is always the possibility that the universe, or our galaxy, or our solar system, could explode at 8 o'clock tonight for a reason or reasons unknown. Highly unlikely, I should think, yet there remains the possibility, and for this reason when we speak of certainties and of events that *must* happen, we must make allowance for it. It is demanded by logic rather than by science.

We might imagine the future as a vast, black and empty space directly in front of us, for that is what I believe it to be – a realm that does not in reality exist. Into that space we might mentally project certain events that must occur from a human perspective. These could include the continued rotation of Earth, the motion of the moon, Earth's orbit around the sun, and various other astronomical events of our own choosing. These are the foundation of our human future in this world. But what else can we be certain of? If we are religious we might believe that God ordains particular events that absolutely nothing could interfere with and allows prophets an insight regarding them. Or we might believe that the law of karma will reward or punish us for the deeds we have performed today or yesterday and that such consequences have been programmed to manifest at some opportune point in time to come; and yet this is all very vague, even if true, and can hardly be plotted, as can the planets. If you are not of a religious persuasion you will probably reject such ideas and might struggle to think of anything that *must* occur, other than that which science has convinced you of.

But just how far into the future should we look? The exact positions of the planets and the stars can be plotted aeons in advance, but that does not guarantee that these bodies will actually be there at those precise times. They will only be there should nothing else occur in the meantime to interfere with their positions. Even science, then, can offer us at best only a highly probable future, not an absolute future. It is not the real future. The real future only exists when it becomes the certainty of the present, the now, and so it is not really the future at all.

Perhaps, however (yet mindful of the above caveat), there are some events which *must* occur because they have reached a critical tipping point and no human intervention or other agency whatever can now prevent them? Perhaps all the components of the event are now so far advanced in assembly that the event is imminent and irresistible? If we return to Eryl Mai Jones's premonition regarding the slag heap and the school, I would argue that it was a type 2 premonition (if premonition it was) which became a type 3, a *may* happen which became a *must* happen, or more accurately, that the *event* was a may happen which became a must happen.

Of course, the manner in which such knowledge could be obtained via a dream invites further speculation, which I shall be glad to embark upon shortly. But first, let us return to the premonition of the Aberfan Disaster and consider how we might begin to explain it, on the assumption that it was indeed 'seen' in advance of the event.

The slag heap which took so many lives was built on a hillside and on top of a stream. It had been raining heavily and a colliery worker had noticed that the heap had reduced significantly in height on the day before the disaster and had sunk even further on the morning the disaster occurred. It was obvious at this point that the slag heap was on the move. I would argue that if a team of experts with sensors and probes and various other bits and pieces had examined the slag heap 24 or even 48 hours before it raced down the hill, they might have been able to predict its collapse to within a few days. By calculating the dimensions and weight of the heap, the amount of rainfall upon it, the flooding of the stream beneath it, the incline of the hill, and so on and so forth, a prediction of its imminent total collapse would be possible. The experts would further be able to calculate its speed, direction and the distance it would cover before finally coming to a halt. No doubt they would also be able to predict with some confidence that the local junior school would be in great danger. However, I do doubt whether such experts would be able to pinpoint with any degree of accuracy the exact hour at which such an event would take place. How, then, could little Eryl Mai Jones have gained knowledge that the school would be occupied at the time of its collapse?

A Universal Consciousness

This is the point at which we must take a leap of imagination and be willing – if only temporarily – to suspend any hard and fast views we may hold regarding the nature of our universe.

One of the greatest of all mysteries is the nature and origin of consciousness. According to many, though not all, scientists, human consciousness is nothing other than the product of electrochemical activity within the brain cells. It is the physical body, they assert, that gives rise to consciousness, and consciousness is therefore extinguished when the physical body dies. The inspiration which it is claimed produces the world's greatest art, music, literature – and even some of the major breakthroughs in science – owes its existence not to some exalted source beyond the confines of the brain, but to the brain's 'anatomy and physiology, and nothing more' as Carl Sagan asserted. The Nobel Laureate Francis Crick, who jointly discovered the structure of DNA in 1962, wrote: 'You, your joys and your sorrows, your memories and ambitions, your sense of personal identity and free will, are in fact no more than the behaviour of a vast assembly of nerve cells and their associated molecules.'

Where Crick's 'in fact' has come from is a mystery, since it is not a proven fact. Perhaps we should always be respectful towards the opinions of accomplished scientists because of the depth of learning that underlies such pronouncements, but they are just that – opinions. Science's greatest practitioners should not attempt to use their pre-eminence to stifle a still ongoing investigation. They should not allow their personal beliefs to intrude upon their professional need for objectivity.

The trap that I may unwittingly fall into in advancing my ideas regarding the basis for precognition is that I, too, may close my mind to other possibilities. So let me state here and now that, yes, I am defending the principle of free-will against the idea of a pre-established future. But perhaps there are other factors that I have not considered and which need to enter into the equation. Therefore, whilst my mind is to some degree already made up, I like to think that nonetheless it is still open to other more persuasive arguments or evidence. In other words, show me something better and I shall happily embrace it. I believe this to be a healthy, progressive attitude.

It may well be that the human consciousness *is* produced by little more than the electricity and chemicals in the human equivalent of a rather large battery. However, an alternative view is that consciousness does not owe its existence to a physical body but to another (I shall refrain from saying 'higher') source. This view holds that the universe itself is conscious. Give this universal consciousness the name God, the Cosmic, the Universal Mind, or any other designation you choose, the claim is that consciousness is independent of – though not entirely distinct from – the physical universe. The physical body plays host to a small portion of this consciousness (as a television set plays host to a television signal) which, upon the body's death, returns to its universal source in some form or other.

Should this latter position be correct, and not the former, then it becomes easier to understand how the phenomenon known as precognition (and perhaps other, related phenomena, collectively known as *psi*) could occur. An omnipresent consciousness that permeates every atom, every molecule, every cell, every single thing in the universe, would be aware of everything, would know everything. Nothing could escape its attention. However, it might be unwise to imagine this universal consciousness as being like some sort of personal god or goddess, sitting around and taking note of what is going on and forming judgements about this, that and the other. Rather, it could be imagined in its ordinary functioning as being more like an automatic process – as data collection, if you will – and as efficient and dispassionate as a computer, though infinitely more intelligent. That this consciousness may have a 'higher' manifestation that 'thinks' about the issues and events of the universe (God?) is an entirely different matter and goes beyond what is necessary for our present purposes.

The world of quantum mechanics is very strange, with scientists of today taking in their stride very many phenomena that would have been considered insane little more than a century ago, such as the ability of a particle to be in two places simultaneously. It is surely therefore only a foolish person who would insist that consciousness could not have pre-existed biological life, since scientifically it is not yet clear what consciousness actually is. It may well be that, at some point in the future, scientists will discover that a universal consciousness necessarily must always have existed and that it is intimately engaged with the quantum world, amongst other things. Or maybe not. But let us speculate nonetheless. We might consider that science is but the universe getting to know itself; and who knows, perhaps one day an understanding of unusual phenomena might sit very comfortably within science's circumference.

If such a condition of universal consciousness were to be a reality rather than merely a hypothesis, it is conceivable that all data regarding the slag heap at Aberfan would be available and 'known' to it. Moreover, the 'team of experts with their sensors and probes' would not even begin to approximate the depth of insight and precision regarding the heap's instability that this universal consciousness would have at its command. Therefore, when young Eryl Mai Jones went to sleep, perhaps her own individual consciousness contacted more intimately and efficiently the greater universal consciousness of which it was a part, and in so doing attuned with the dreadful scenario which would later unfold (if nothing or no one were to intervene). But whether such knowledge of the 'future' would be obtained by Eryl Mai Jones accidentally or by design is open to yet more speculation.

Again, it must be emphasised that this hypothesis does not imply that the tragedy that befell Aberfan was inevitable. At the time of Eryl Mai Jones's dream, just over twenty four hours before it occurred, it was perhaps inevitable that the slag heap would soon collapse and run its destructive course, and that it was far too late now to do anything to prevent it. However, it was not inevitable that its collapse would bring about the death of so many human beings, since with adequate warning the village could have been evacuated. But since when did a little girl's nightmare qualify as an adequate warning?

The Woman in the Tree

Imagine, if you will, a very tall tree with a woman sitting on its topmost branch. This woman is favoured with an excellent overview of all things beneath her. A car has been parked on a hill, but its handbrake is faulty, so the car begins to roll down the road, at such an angle that it will mount the pavement at exactly the spot where several children are playing with their toys. The woman in the tree shouts, 'Watch out for the car!' But she is too far distant from the children to be heard by them.

Meanwhile, the car is steadily picking up speed and will soon be hurtling directly at the children. However, the father of one of the group, who is relaxing in his front garden, catches sight of the distant woman in the tree. He, too, cannot hear her crying out, but he does register the fact that she is frantically waving and pointing. Curious as to what is going on, he steps out of his garden to take a closer look. He spies the car, hurriedly grabs the children, pulls them into the garden – and averts a certain disaster.

Beneath a different aspect of the tree is a giant maze, with its hedges so high that the woman inside it cannot see over them, even if she jumps. She is seeking the exit, but is totally lost and increasingly desperate. An hour later and she is still lost. She calls out for help. The woman in the tree has noticed her predicament and shouts down some helpful instructions: 'Turn left, then right, then ...' But the woman in the maze has not heard her. Even when she thinks she can hear a voice, she believes she has imagined it and so ignores it. She fails to raise her eyes beyond the top of the hedges that surround her on all sides and thereby fails to see the great tree that towers above her, in which a helpful woman sits. She struggles on, crying out for help, whilst deliberately blocking out the faint voice of guidance that from time to time she discerns.

Perhaps the woman in the tree bears some resemblance to the universal consciousness, if such exists? The woman sees all, knows all, tries to help when help is needed, but often isn't heard, or seen, or believed, or understood. The father in the garden received only a faint and vague indication of something untoward, yet it was sufficient to capture his attention and for him to take action and prevent a calamity. Perhaps some precognitive experiences are similarly faint and vague and this is why they do not always have a happy outcome? The woman in the maze who craved guidance heard and yet ignored it when it was given. Perhaps, similarly, human beings often ignore their inner intuitive promptings and thereby often stumble their way through life? Perhaps one day this universal consciousness will turn out to be not just a hypothesis but a reality and then everyone will give the woman in the tree a big, enthusiastic wave?

An Unusual Case

In 2007, Channel 5 broadcast a documentary titled, *The Man Who Dreams The Future*. Its subject was Chris Robinson, who is reputed to be a lucid dreamer; that is to say, he allegedly has the ability to pose questions while awake which will be answered in a dream the very same night. Robinson claims to have 'seen' in his dreams various traumatic future events, including the suicide of his father-in-law, the destruction of the twin towers in New York on 9/11, and the London bombings of 7/7.

Professor Chris French, of the Anomalous Psychology Unit,

University of London, conducted an experiment with Robinson in which six different locations in London were chosen; Robinson then had to dream which of the six he and French were to visit the following day. Robinson had no prior knowledge of any of the locations, and which of them they were to visit was to be determined randomly by the roll of a dice on the morning in question, and then only *after* the details of the dream had been recorded. An independent observer would decide which of the six locations the dream most closely matched. If the match and the dice produced the same location, then Robinson would be deemed to have scored a 'hit'. This procedure was to be repeated three times in order to avoid the possibility of coincidence.

On day one, in the film, Robinson reports dreaming of paint, and of white sheets. The independent observer quite reasonably matches these details to Number 2, the House of Dreams, which is the home of a painter. However, when the dice is rolled the location to be visited is Number 4, the Ice Bar, a cocktail bar made entirely of ice. When Robinson's blindfold is removed at this location he says that it cannot be argued that he isn't surrounded by white. However, Professor French protests that he thinks it is actually quite dark in there (it is) and is worried that, whatever location they had visited, Robinson would say that, ah, now that's why I dreamt this … and so on, and would find some element or other in his dream which matched up with that place. French declares this first test a 'miss'.

On day two, Robinson reports rolling or unrolling something – it could be in a printing works. On his notepad we can read 'Blue carbon paper … duplicate book … print-ink'. The independent observer matches this dream to location Number 1, St. Bride's Crypt just off Fleet Street, which has historic links to the printing industry, but the dice brings up location 5, a city farm. Both French and Robinson agree that this is definitely a 'miss'.

On the third and final day, Robinson dreams of 'dead people'.

The independent observer matches this once again to St. Bride's Crypt, and the roll of the dice also brings up St. Bride's Crypt. The two men visit and encounter, amongst other things, piles of human bones. French declares this dream a 'hit'. Overall, however, the experiment is regarded by him as a failure.

Now it seems to me that French was correct in his assessment of the experiment as far as precognition is concerned. However, it does seem very evident that Robinson demonstrated substantial ability of some other kind. I would argue that Robinson was 'tuning in' to the knowledge of the six locations held by the independent observer. During his dreams, Robinson picked up on several of the components of these locations:

1. The white sheets. Robinson did not claim to be surrounded by *light*, either in his dream or while in the Ice Bar, so French was wrong to argue that it was quite dark in there. Yes, it was moderately dark, yet it was very plain to the viewer that the walls were white. The ice was reflecting the light that was available, and thus appeared white.
2. Paint. Robinson picked up on the fact that one location was the house of a painter.
3. The several references to the printing industry. St. Bride's Church, in London, has for hundreds of years been associated with newspapers.
4. Dead people. Robinson was spot on.

From the evidence of the documentary, I can't tell if Robinson recorded any references to the other locations that were not visited. But what he did perceive during his dreams does seem to be of significance. Yet I contend that he was not seeing the future, only gaining knowledge of locations which had *already* been determined; that is to say, in his dreams Robinson was tuning in to the mind of the independent observer who was aware of each of the six locations.

The throw of the dice was always the element that was bound to cause him problems. That his third dream matched up brilliantly with the dice location was, I would argue, itself just a happy coincidence which could very easily have ended up as another 'miss'. Robinson was dreaming of a *potential* future, not the actual future, in the sense that any of these locations *could* have been selected by the dice to be visited. A more careful experiment of this type would omit the pre-selected locations. In their place, perhaps a stranger could be picked from the street once the dream has been recorded … and asked to stick a pin in a very large map! Genuine premonition of an actual future would be able to handle such randomness.

As for the dream regarding his father-in-law's suicide, which occurred several days before the event, I would suggest that Robinson had somehow peered into the man's troubled mind as he contemplated or planned his own death by hanging. Robinson saw not the future death, but the *planned* future death of his father-in-law, perhaps through the medium of our hypothetical universal consciousness.

The dream regarding the events of 9/11, to which allegedly there were several witnesses when it was reported, I would again argue was not a glimpse of the future. Rather, Robinson peered into the minds of those who had been plotting the atrocities and who were now relishing the probable outcomes. The dream occurred just a few days prior to 9/11 and those terrorists who were 'in the know' regarding the plans were undoubtedly feeling strong emotions and projecting strong visualizations in regard to their future deeds, and perhaps these could manifest quite powerfully within a universal consciousness, which possibly is where Chris Robinson accessed them.

TIME TRAVEL

At long last your time machine is completed following many years of research, design, development and seemingly endless secret toil. The final rivet has been hammered in and the entire, strange contraption is now receiving its final polish. You are eager to take your machine on its first ever test-flight, or drive, or spin, or whatever a time machine actually does as it encounters the past or the future. For the 'maiden voyage' you have decided that you would like to travel back in time to meet the great-grandfather you never knew, the great-grandfather who died long before you were born. You have heard many fascinating stories about him and have concluded that it would be of enormous personal benefit to you to meet this remarkable and wonderful man at different stages in his life. The house in which he lived for much of that life is still standing, and is just a mile or two away, so you set your coordinates accordingly, to 'land' in his parlour, as it was possibly then called. Following much reflection, you have decided to first visit your relative when he was a young man, immediately prior to him leaving to fight in the Great War. You want to know how he feels about it. So, you turn the dial to the required date.

You have one or two concerns, however. If your contraption suddenly appears in front of your great-grandfather as he sits serenely smoking his pipe, the shock of seeing it emerging ghost-like out of nothingness could bring on a heart-attack and kill him. Or, your somewhat bulky machine might alight upon his head and squash him to death. Either event would not really be welcome, not for your great-grandfather and not for you, since his premature death, before he had even met your great-grandmother, would inevitably mean that you would never have been born.

So how is it that you have just travelled back in time and killed him?

This is a typical paradoxical scenario that arises when time travel to the past is considered. Einstein's revolutionary discoveries in physics have inevitably thrown up even more problems for us to contend with.

It has been suggested that you could go back in time and, at the appropriate moment, tell a young Einstein all about the theory of relativity that you have learned from studying his life and works. Thus Einstein – earlier than previously, and with minimal effort – can now proceed to 'discover' and develop relativity. Many years later, of course, and back in your own time, you will read about his discovery and then go back in time to inform Einstein of it. A strange loop has been created. Who is the true discoverer of relativity? In this scenario it would appear that no one did – neither Einstein nor you. You learnt it from him and he learnt it from you. Could such a trick as this *really* be possible?

But why give the theory of relativity to Einstein? Why not have a little chat with Isaac Newton and give the theory to him and let him steal all the glory, since Einstein is destined to upstage him in years to come? The trouble is, if Newton does manage to grasp all these strange new concepts far ahead of their time, and does manage to publish them and gain recognition and fame for them, what will poor old Einstein occupy himself with when eventually he comes along? Perhaps he will become more accomplished on his violin or call to see the Barber of Seville for a decent haircut?

All of this theoretical mucking about with history, and with events that are supposedly fixed, perhaps reach beyond the paradoxical to the nonsensical. Again, there is speculation that we could step out of our time machine and meet our younger self. Everything sounds so very easy. If so, why not go back to meet yourself as you were, say, five years ago, then both of you enter the time machine and go further back in time to collect yourself as you were ten years ago, then fifteen, then … There are now five of you, all sitting down together, enjoying a nice cup of tea and a biscuit and discussing the marvels of science and of how well things have turned out for you in life, what with this wonderful time machine, and … and all the while descending ever more certainly into the absurd? In which of the five versions of 'you' will your consciousness be located? Through which of these five pairs of eyes will you be looking out upon the world? Or will you be viewing the world through all five pairs simultaneously?

The past is the past. It is fixed. Non-negotiable. Immutable. History is not like a film on DVD that we can easily and endlessly rewind and then somehow enter into and participate in. If we *were* able to do this then we would corrupt the film, we would destroy its integrity. If we were able to visit the past – not just in imagination and speculatively, but physically, in person – we would corrupt that past and, because *we* are there, render it in some sense part of the future: malsequence.

Nor is the past like some distant country that we can easily hop on a plane to visit. Travel to the past presupposes that somewhere out there, right 'now', there is King Henry VIII of England still acting out his life and scheming to rid himself of yet another wife; that the pyramids are still being built; that dinosaurs are still roaming the Earth.

I shall offer a reason why I think they are not.

A Madeira Cake

Let us return to the reality of your very own time machine. You wish to visit your great-grandfather but do not wish to knock him down dead, neither through shock nor collision. Plus, upon reflection, you still are not too sure whether your machine is truly safe for you to travel in: will you be able to get back to the present in one piece? Or for that matter, will you be able to get to the past in one piece?

You have an ingenious solution. You have heard that your great-grandfather, Tom, was a lover of all things sweet – especially cakes. Therefore, why not send a cake on the maiden voyage, with a note to accompany it, asking Tom to send a message back commenting on whether or not he enjoyed the confection, and attaching his signature? He should then press the button marked 'Return' and the time machine will then, unsurprisingly, return. In this way, you would be able to tell if the cake had arrived safely and could verify from the signature that it was indeed great-grandfather Tom whom you (or rather, your cake) had actually contacted.

You hurriedly build a mini-time machine that is big enough to hold a cake, yet small enough to avoid obliterating your great-grandfather should it accidentally drop out of the future onto his head.

Now for the cake. A Madeira cake. Self-raising flour, butter, caster sugar, eggs. No lemon essence – not sure your great-grandfather would want all these fine ingredients to be blotted out by any unnecessary flavourings. You mix and bake the cake. You wait impatiently for it to cool down, lest the heat should interfere with the machine's delicate instrumentation or with your great-grandfather's delicate palate.

The countdown begins. (There is no reason for a countdown, when all you have to do is press the green button marked 'Go', but it all adds to the sense of drama and the significance of the occasion.) You say your farewells to the cake, wish it a safe and comfortable journey, close the door, 3, 2, 1, pray, press the green button and the machine and the cake are gone. Miraculous! A triumph!

You can't help but reflect on the fate of the cake. Will the machine judder during its journey so that the cake becomes a pile of crumbs? How long will the machine take to reach its destination? Maybe there will be lots of time-warps and things to negotiate and the cake could therefore be stale, or at the very least dry and unappetising, upon arrival, in which case there could be a very nasty letter of complaint from your great-grandfather about certain supposedly edible and tasty goods not being quite up to scratch, etc.

You wait. And wait. And wait some more. The tension is really starting to get to you. A day goes by. A week. A month. Nothing. You are now tearing your hair out with worry. Did the cake survive and arrive? Has it been eaten by your great-grandfather but he simply can't be bothered to reply? Is he in reality but an ungrateful greedy-guts who has sold your time machine for scrap? So many imponderables. Should you personally visit in the full-size time machine to get some answers? Is it safe to do so? *Where, O where, is the cake?*

A Kaleidoscope

Imagine a kaleidoscope with all its coloured plastic pieces, its mirrors, and all the wonderful patterns it makes as you turn it round and view it through the eyepiece. The same plastic pieces, the same mirrors, produce all these very different and unique patterns. The universe is something like a kaleidoscope, though obviously on a far grander scale. Since the Big Bang, 13.7 billion years ago, all the bits and pieces of the universe have always existed in one form or another and are constantly being re-arranged into new and unique 'patterns', we might say. Haven't the cosmologists told us that we human beings are all made – literally – from stardust? If we think about it, everything that constitutes our physical bodies has been through seemingly endless permutations with other forms of energy or matter. We are 100% recycled goods! All the constituents of our cells originated somewhere other than in ourselves.

What has all of this to do with our long-lost cake? Well, if time-travel to the past really is to work, then we really must travel back authentically; that is to say, if we go back one hundred years then we must expect to experience conditions as they really were one hundred years ago throughout the universe. The *universe*, not just planet Earth. The photons that constitute sunlight, moonlight, starlight, would have to revert to what and where they were at that time. Planets would be in different places. Galaxies that are now hurtling through space would have to occupy their previous positions.

If our Madeira cake, in its bespoke time machine, travels back in time and time only, then when it completes its journey it will no longer be on planet Earth but somewhere billions of miles away from our planet floating about in space. This is because Earth, apart from revolving on its axis and moving in orbit around the sun, also travels very rapidly through space together with all other constituents of our galaxy, the Milky Way. Therefore, inevitably, the cake will be located in that part of space which is occupied by Earth *now*, the moment it departed, whereas the Earth of one hundred years ago has yet to arrive in that same location – it is billions of miles farther back.

It is essential, then, that the time machine is additionally able to double up as a spaceship. If it cannot, it cannot return to a meaningful past. The time machine must also be able to far exceed the speed at which Earth travels. If it can only *match* the speed of Earth, it would take far too long to travel back in time one hundred years, by which time its occupant would possibly be dead. Therefore, the time machine-come-spaceship must be able to travel at a very great speed in order to make the venture viable. Since Earth, together with our galaxy, hurtles through space at around 40,000 miles per hour (according to some calculations: it seems to vary depending on which source you consult!), and the fastest manned spacecraft so far built travelled at around 25,000 miles per hour, there needs to be quite a leap in technological development if the time machine is going to cover the 35 billion miles in a reasonably short period. In a thousand years' time, if one of your descendants wishes to visit you, his ancestor, he shall have to travel approximately

350 billion miles in order to do so and will need one helluva fast vehicle!

There also arises the question as to whether a person travelling back through time could himself continue to go forward in time. By this I mean that his heart and all other bodily functions will be expected to operate as normal, moving towards his body's 'future', and yet that very same body will outwardly and in every sense be involved in some kind of time reversal. Are the two compatible? Even if the transition from the present to the past were to be an instantaneous jump, rather than a gradual journey, there seems to be an anomaly. A paradox?

Motion, Space and Consciousness

But we still need to ask whether our time machine really could travel to the past, even if it did possess these advanced capabilities. Time is not some mysterious energy that flows back and forth and which can be distorted and played around with. Time does not exist in and of itself. Time is intimately associated with space, yes, as in space-time, but it is also intimately associated with movement, motion. Our days and years are based on the motion of the Earth relative to the Sun, our months on the motion of the Moon relative to the Earth. Even our incredibly accurate atomic clocks are dependent upon the motion of atoms of the element caesium. All of this is stating the obvious, and yet the obvious is often overlooked when travel through time is contemplated. It may well be possible for light and other energies to go backwards or forwards in time in a local sense, and in a relative sense, but for a human being to experience the events of one hundred years ago as they *authentically* were, may involve a very major upheaval. Would the universe itself have to be the time machine – operating in 'reverse gear'?

After all, the future of one hundred years from now will involve the movement of the components of the whole universe in 'forward gear', so why should access to the past involve a different type of mechanism? Time – forwards or backwards – is dependent upon *motion*, and possesses no particular power of its own. Could it really be possible to travel to the future when the universe itself has not yet done so?

Consciousness, too, must play its part as a component of what we call time. There is no time without consciousness, without awareness. Perhaps there may exist *sequence*, but it is consciousness which converts this sequence into the phenomenon we call time. Motion through space + consciousness = time? Our old friend Gödel supposedly demonstrated that time, as an independent force in a relativistic universe, could not exist. Could he be right?

Where is the cake?

So, what really *did* happen to the cake? If it is assumed that the cake has to go through every second in 'reverse gear' in order to reach the past, just as it had to go through every second in 'forward gear' in order to become a cake, then if you were able to observe this process you would witness some astonishing events. You would see the self-raising flour used to make the cake temporarily return to its packet in the kitchen cupboard. The eggs and butter would return to the fridge. The caster sugar would be packed away, too. But, if you watched a little longer, you'd see them all disappear. Where did they go? To the supermarket from which you bought them. Then where? Well, the eggs are being created inside three different hens. The flour is now inside a distribution warehouse. The butter is in a large box in the back of a lorry that is travelling on a motorway towards the supermarket. Skip five years and where are your eggs now? Where are the other ingredients? Answer: unrecognizable for what they once were, and in thousands – if not millions, or billions – of different places. Some of the water molecules in your eggs are floating in a lovely cloud in the sky. Some are making their way down a river. The hens that laid your eggs have not even been hatched yet. At the moment, your butter has not yet become the grass that becomes the milk.

Many years ago, components of your cake were still to arrive from the Sun. Many of your cake's water molecules were currently enjoying life in the cells of insects, animals and human beings. So, your cake that is travelling from the future can do one of two things if it is to really and truly and authentically inhabit this world of a century ago: it can arrive intact as the splendid, highly desirable confection you created, in which case billions of living and non-living things from that day and age will have parts of themselves ripped out in order to facilitate this; or, the cake will have to be ripped apart, atom by molecule, in order to ensure that these other things *are not* compromised in any way. An authentic past would seem to demand the latter option, since one hundred years ago there was no such cake in existence and all its components were, in fact, elsewhere to be found. Your cake, therefore, has disintegrated, together with the time machine itself. You, too, will be shattered into billions of pieces if you attempt to follow your cake, for you, too, are recycled. Your various bits and pieces were around when your great-grandfather was alive, and were around long before that. You are not some independent being that can roam time and the universe without consequence.

If you wish to travel from one place to another, then this traversal of space will also involve an expenditure of time and motion. So why, when we contemplate journeying through time, do we often overlook the essential contribution of space and motion? We cannot isolate time to the exclusion of these other two. The three are irrevocably interlinked.

There is a similarity here to the relationship that exists between the three dimensions of space. If we draw a horizontal line, thus, _____ we cannot say that this is solely one-dimensional. Despite the preponderance of length, the line does still possess a degree of the second dimension, breadth, otherwise we wouldn't be able to see it, or, perhaps more accurately, it couldn't be drawn. Furthermore, the third dimension also participates in the line's structure, since the ink or whatever else of which it is composed has depth. There are no entities that are solely one-dimensional or two-dimensional: where the one dimension exists, so do the other two, always and forever. They are a part of the fabric of our universe and cannot be split off into separate or discrete units.

Professor Stephen Hawking posits a Chronology Protection Agency, some sort of cosmological mechanism which prevents travel to the past. He argues that the greatest evidence there is for this is the total absence of tourists visiting us from the future. Well, yes, I believe there is such a mechanism, and it is the simple fact that those potential tourists are already here, or at least all of their physical components are (I shall omit from this discussion the possible existence of a soul, as it will only serve to complicate matters even further). It is no real argument to say that a tourist from the future will be composed of the *future* manifestation of these atoms, molecules, particles, so those in the present will remain unaffected. If such *is* the argument, then we could extrapolate by saying that the glass of water before me now is not the same one as the exact same one I am observing ten minutes later, and ten minutes after that, and ten minutes after that. If this theory of time travel proved to be true, we could collect up all these water molecules from every ten minute interval until a billion years into the future and bring them all together at one time to form a lovely ocean to swim in. But I would advise you not to dive in to it as you may bump your head! Surely we are not postulating the existence of an infinite number of near-duplicate universes, that the universe of ten minutes hence is entirely distinct from the one I am inhabiting in the present, the *now*?

Let us consider the pyramids. The Great Pyramid at Giza has straddled the best part of four and a half thousand years. All around it, the world has been changing – *moving* – while the pyramid itself has remained virtually the same. Granted, blocks of stone have been removed from its sides, human beings have smashed their way in, and erosion has taken its toll; and yet the greater bulk remains intact. The atoms that compose the stone are the same atoms that composed the stone on the very day the pyramid was completed – and indeed, they go back much further than that! Time for these atoms has in some sense stood still, since they have not altered much in their relation to other atoms and energies in the pyramid for a very long period. If we plucked out one of the pyramid's atoms now and sent it back over four thousand years in time to 'meet' itself as it was then, what would happen? Could these two atoms, younger and older, stand side by side, as it were, and compare notes?

The answer I would suggest is, No, they could not be placed side by side. As with the cake, the atom from the present would disappear and become the atom of the past, for the two are one and the same. Also, introducing an atom to the past, even if it was only one, would surely cause great upset if it was additional to the sum total of all atoms that existed at that past moment? The past was all sorted and arranged, and a surplus of just one more atom that was not there previously would have a knock-on effect for everything else that existed at the time. Would there not be a violation of the law of conservation of energy, which states that energy can neither be created nor destroyed? Wouldn't just one atom from the future, which is added to the sum total of that which existed in the past, be equivalent to creation?

Chaos theory asserts that a butterfly flapping its wings in Europe could cause a hurricane in the Caribbean. By this it is meant that there could be something like a chain reaction, begun in a very small way, that snowballs to ever greater effect and consequence. So, illegitimately to insert our atom into the past, where it exists already, would be to push something else out of the way, which would follow suit, and so on, almost endlessly. Very quickly the authentic past would disintegrate, and so therefore would the future, including our present.

Is this ever likely to happen? Perhaps not. Because as we have previously suggested, the universe itself may have to act as the time machine and go into reverse, and this is most unlikely to happen. Even if it did, the atom from the present would soon revert to its former role. There are no younger and older versions of the same atoms, in infinite series, just ageless atoms, and there is only one version of each.

The Paradox of the Twins

We have learned from Einstein that time is relative, that it passes at different rates according to our frame of reference. A man who has travelled in a spaceship at a rate approaching the speed of light may return home to discover that his twin brother has aged fifty years more than him. Faster speeds and/or longer journeys through space may result in hundreds or thousands of years having passed when eventually he returns home. Such a phenomenon may indeed strike us as being a form of time travel, and undoubtedly it is. However, at no point does our space traveller depart the universe, able almost instantaneously to appear either in the future or in the past. From Earth, it would theoretically be possible to keep track of the spaceship wherever it might go (unless, perhaps, it disappeared into a black hole!).

What does happen is that, relative to his brother, the space traveller's whole biological system drastically slows down, due to the tremendous speed at which he is travelling. All of his organs, the thoughts he is thinking – everything – now function at a far, far slower rate than when he was on Earth, and because his mental processes themselves are so much slower, he is unable to detect any difference. Everything about himself is exactly as normal, from his perspective. But isn't this phenomenon more to do with motion than to do with time? Both men exist in the same universe concurrently, even though due to relativity they may experience it in a somewhat different way.

Final Thoughts

As suggested earlier, if a man was travelling backwards in time, his heart and all of his other organs would naturally still need to move *forwards* in time in order for him to function correctly and normally as a human being. This does seem to be an anomaly, a paradox. That is why I believe that if we really could put time into reverse, we would also put out bodies into reverse and begin to disintegrate. The forward motion of time has collected all the elements of our bodies together and I believe the backward motion of time would put these elements back where they came from.

I am not convinced by the suggestion of physics that you could travel in a normal, 'forwards' way along a 'closed time-like curve' that takes you without any hitches to the past. While such a fortuitous route may indeed exist, for the moment it sounds just a little too convenient. Other objections are overcome by the 'multiverse' theory, which proposes that an infinite number of universes may exist in parallel with our own. By this account, it would be possible to travel back in time, though not to our own past, but to that of an almost identical universe. Here we would be free to make different choices to those we made previously and there would additionally be no violation of the law of the conservation of energy. However, even if such a multiverse does exist, going back in time to a universe other than our own *does not* constitute the 'true' time travel that some of its advocates claim for it. Rather, this seems more like a cop-out. If we cannot journey to our own past but only to one that is very similar, then we have done little other than side-step the issue. This is not authentic time travel but a second best alternative.

It seems to me that there is a relentless sequence that is always moving in a single, 'forwards' direction, and that it is the *motion* of *energy* and *matter* through *space* that is the most salient and significant feature of this process, not time, which is but a *measurement* or awareness of it.

I believe that the past has irretrievably gone. It has gone into the present. It will proceed into the future. Every last piece and particle of former times is here with us now. All the atoms that constituted King Henry VIII throughout his lifetime are still here and some have moved on to comprise part of some new person or some new thing. Before Henry was born all those billions of particles led separate 'lives', until they became concentrated in close proximity in the one body, the one man, some for a very short time, some for quite a while longer, but eventually all were (and still are being) dispersed and went on their individual way, probably never again to congregate in such manner. They are *not* still out there, in some science-fiction past or present, living and re-living the life of Henry over and over again, ad infinitum, and available for limitless visits and interference from the future.

Matter and energy in motion is all there is, with inputs from many sources – including human beings – directing them into new configurations, changing them into this and that. The future is but one, or two, or three turns of the kaleidoscope. Motion is the key, not time. Time is a measurement and not a thing in itself; it is without substance. If motion ceases, time stops. Time is an interval between events that are the product of motion, and is wholly dependent upon consciousness. The future exists, and always has existed, but only as a potential state that is forever brewing.

Remove consciousness from the equation and, I would assert, time then reduces to nothing other than *sequence*. And time travel, I believe, necessarily involves *mal*sequence, that is, a violation of the established cosmic order; therefore it cannot be possible.

(I think.)

FURTHER RESEARCH

As mentioned in the preface, I present below some further questions that have arisen as a consequence of my analyses, and which the reader may wish to attempt to resolve for him or herself.

1. With reference to the true/false trichotomy, we can test a proposition and demonstrate that the *either true or false* claim is correct. Also, we fail to successfully test a Gödel sentence and thereby demonstrate that the *neither true nor false* claim is correct. However, when we test the Liar paradox we *do not* demonstrate that the *both true and false* claim is correct. Rather, we say such a condition is impossible, that all we in fact achieve is neutrality, or *neither true nor false*. What is going on here?

2. We have produced a question equivalent of the Liar, the Q-Liar, but can there be a question equivalent of the Gödel sentence – a Q-Gödel? An equation equivalent – the E-Gödel?

3. In the Barber of Seville and Russell's Paradox, we identified a *forbidden third*, a third group which interferes with the two polar opposites to create paradox. But could a paradox be devised which includes a *forbidden fourth*, or even a *forbidden fifth*?

GLOSSARY

Disproof (See *Verification moment*)

Excluded middle, Law of
This law states that a proposition must be either true or false and there cannot be anything in between.

Forbidden third
A third group or element which is introduced into a pair of polar opposites to create a paradox. This third group is 'forbidden' because it is different in composition from both of the polar opposites and is therefore impossible to align with either of them. It does not belong.

Gödel sentence
A statement that is eternally neutral (not undecidable). Because it cannot be proved or disproved, it cannot be true or false. As the second member of the true/false trichotomy it is, 'This statement is neither true nor false'. As Gödel constructed it, it is, 'This statement cannot be proved or disproved'. A Gödel sentence *is not* a proposition.

Malsequence
When a fixed stage in a particular sequence has been displaced to occupy another (usually earlier) stage, this is malsequence. The sequence could, for example, be natural, logical, temporal, or a combination of these. A natural example of malsequence might be *pip-apple* rather than *pip-tree-blossom-apple*. A mathematical example

might be *1 2 3 4 7 5 6 8*. Of course, such a condition cannot really exist, but we can be fooled into thinking it can – and this can give rise to paradox.

Non-contradiction, Law of
This law states that a proposition cannot be both true *and* false.

Paradox
See definitions in the preface.

Predicate (See *Proposition*)

Primary content
This is the content of a sentence that affirms or denies something and is the sole reason for the proposition existing at all. It comprises a *subject* and a *predicate*. Secondary content is a proposition's implicit assertion of its own truthfulness, which may or may not be the case. For example, with "The door is open", what really matters is whether or not the door *is* open; it is the status of the door that is the *primary* focus of our attention, and so this is the sentence's primary content. Whether the proposition is true or false is of *secondary* concern, and so this is the sentence's secondary content.

Primary knowledge
Primary knowledge results when *primary content* has been successfully tested, to give us proof or disproof. See *verification moment*.

Proof (See *Verification moment*)

Proposition
The content of a sentence that affirms or denies something and is capable of being true or false. A proposition comprises a subject and

a predicate. For example, in "The door is open", the subject is the door and the predicate is what is claimed regarding the door, ie. that it is open. A proposition is the first of three types of statement in the true/false trichotomy.

Secondary content (See *Primary content*)

Secondary knowledge
Secondary knowledge – whether a proposition is true or false – results when primary knowledge (proof or disproof) has been obtained. Proof automatically generates a 'true' and disproof a 'false'.

Subject (See *Proposition*)

Tralse
The fusion of true and false, where both conditions exist at one and the same time. This is the state that the Liar paradox would really achieve, rather than the vicious circularity or oscillation of true, false, true, false, recurring. However, tralse is an impossible state, it cannot exist, and all that would actually be achieved is neutrality – neither true nor false.

Trichotomy
A division into three categories. In the trichotomy of opposites, the polar opposites a and b can be arranged into only three possible groups: 1. either a or b; 2. neither a nor b; 3. both a and b. In the true/false trichotomy, a and b are replaced by true and false and provide the blueprints for 1. a proposition, 2. a Gödel sentence and 3. The Liar paradox.

Verification boundary
The point at which the claim of a proposition is tested. This could be by an experiment, a test, an observation, a calculation, etc. Once

the verification boundary has been crossed, a proposition is transformed into either a fact or a falsehood for the person who has tested it. To anyone else who has not tested it, the proposition remains just that, a proposition, neither true nor false. The verification boundary separates the unknown (proposition) from the known (fact or falsehood).

Verification moment

A mental realization, this is the instant at which we gain *primary knowledge*, when a proposition is either proved or disproved. At this moment, all doubt regarding the claim of a proposition – its *primary content* – is removed and knowledge is obtained. For example, with the proposition, 'The door is open', we observe the door and determine whether it is open or closed. If open, we have proof; if closed, we have disproof. Proof and disproof constitute primary knowledge.

Verification response

A mental realization that a proposition's claim is either true or false. If the claim has been proved, then the response is that the proposition is true; if disproved, the response is that the proposition is false. In the absence of proof or disproof, there can be no true or false response. True and false constitute secondary knowledge.

Verification statement

A written or spoken version of the verification response. For example, in response to 'The door is open', a verification statement will declare this proposition either true or false. The danger is that this could be a lie, so to anyone who reads or hears it, it is no different to a proposition, ie. the statement itself could be either true or false.

FURTHER READING

Al-Khalili, Jim. *Paradox: The Nine Greatest Enigmas in Science*. Bantam Press, London (2010).

Casti, John L. and DePauli, Werner. *Gödel: A Life of Logic*. Perseus Publishing, Cambridge, USA (2000).

Clark, Michael. *Paradoxes from A to Z*. Routledge, London (2002).

Crick, Francis. *The Astonishing Hypothesis*. Simon&Schuster, New York (1994).

Dossey, Larry. *The Power of Premonitions*. Hay House, London (2009).

Falletta, Nicholas. *The Paradoxicon*. Turnstone Press, Wellingborough (1985).

Hughes, Patrick and Brecht, George. *Vicious Circles and Infinity*. Penguin Books, Harmondsworth (1978).

Lynds, Peter. *Zeno's Paradoxes: A Timely Solution*. Philsci Archive (2003).

O'Beirne, T.H. *Can the Unexpected Never Happen?* The New Scientist, pp.464-65 (May 25, 1965).

Parnia, Sam. *What Happens when we Die?* Hay House, London (2005).

Quine, W. V. O. *On a So-Called Paradox*. Mind, 62, p67 (1953).

Russell, Bertrand. *My Philosophical Development*. Spokesman, Nottingham (2007).

Sagan, Carl. *The Dragons of Eden*. Random House, New York (1977).

Sainsbury, R. M. *Paradoxes*. Cambridge University Press, Cambridge (1995).

Salmon, Wesley C. *Space, Time and Motion*. Dickenson Publishing Company, Inc., Encino, California, USA (1975).

Searle, John R. *The Mystery of Consciousness*. Granta Books, London (1998).

Smullyan, Raymond. *What is the Name of this Book?* Penguin Books, London (1981).

Sorensen, Roy. *A Brief History of the Paradox*. Oxford University Press, New York (2003).

Yourgrau, Palle. *A World Without Time*. Penguin Books, London (2007).

INDEX